THE UNITED STATES
AND SAUDI ARABIA

THE MIDDLE EAST

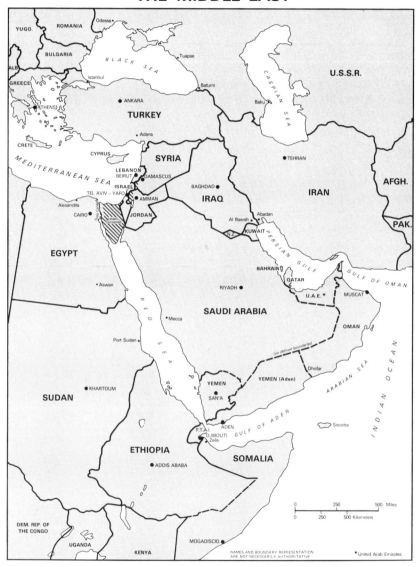

Source: U.S. Department of State, Bureau of Public Affairs, *Special Report: U.S. Policy in the Middle East,* December 1973-November 1974.

THE UNITED STATES AND SAUDI ARABIA

A Policy Analysis

Emile A. Nakhleh

American Enterprise Institute for Public Policy Research
Washington, D. C.

Emile A. Nakhleh is associate professor of political science and chairman of the department of history and political science at Mount Saint Mary's College, Emmitsburg, Maryland.

ISBN 0-8447-3184-6

Foreign Affairs Study 26, October 1975

Library of Congress Catalog Card No. 75-33486

Printed in the United States of America

CONTENTS

INTRODUCTION

Saudi Arabia occupies a unique position in American foreign policy—economically, politically and strategically. Economically, Saudi Arabia is the world's largest oil producer and holds over one-fourth of the world's proven oil reserves. It has a decisive voice in the movement and price structure of oil worldwide. The United States, on the other hand, though it is the second largest oil producer, holds no more than 6 percent of the world's proven oil reserves. At the same time, the United States consumes almost 40 percent of the world's energy, and American imports of oil have continued to rise.

The commercial and military agreement that the United States signed with Saudi Arabia in June 1974 is a definite indication of the paramount economic position of Saudi Arabia in American long-range policy planning. Whether this mutual special relationship is a result of any feasibility studies or whether it is simply a response to an immediate economic need remains to be seen. The important factor is that American policy planners do indeed perceive this special tie as primarily economic.

The United States is also economically interested in the unprecedented sums of petrodollars amassed in Saudi hands, funds which cannot in the near future be absorbed into the Saudi economy. Consequently, since early 1974 American policy makers have consciously endeavored to lure some of these petrodollars back to the United States in the form of short-term investments, investments in United States government bonds or as payments for American services to the Saudi government. One of the easiest methods, and by far the most questionable in terms of long-range planning, is the outright sale of American arms and other military services.

In terms of volume and quality, the arms sold to Saudi Arabia by the United States since early 1974 do not appear to reflect thorough planning and direction by the National Security Council. (This is also true of arms sales to Iran.) It also seems that economic expediency, which has been put forth as the rationale for the sale of these arms, has prevented any serious inquiry into their potential use. The crucial question here is whether the preponderance of highly sophisticated American arms in a very volatile region of the world furthers or undermines American long-range national interest in that region. The lack of an official answer to this question indicates that the politics of arms has yielded to the economics of oil.

The political/ideological dynamics of Saudi Arabia are of considerable importance to American long-range policy in the Middle East in general and in the Arabian peninsula in particular. The evolution of the Saudi political system from an absolute monarchy based on strict observance of Islamic precepts combined with tribal traditions to a more modern form of government has wide-ranging implications to Saudi Arabia and to its neighbors. Beyond the system itself, Saudi political development, whether evolutionary or revolutionary, will have a measurable impact on long-term political stability in the region. Likewise, the stability of United States relations with Saudi Arabia will be influenced by the nature of political reform within the country and by the intensity of present and future political radicalism in the region.

Although tribal political traditionalism has worked fairly successfully in Saudi Arabia so far, internal political reform is inevitable. The new urban, college-educated economic middle class of Saudis is rapidly expanding, and the increasing centralization of government will generate a national—albeit initially elitist—demand for political change before the end of this decade. The nature of the reform and the degree of internal political stability to a large extent will be determined by the ruling family's willingness and ability to identify and respond to the demand for political change. Whatever the outcome, repercussions will be felt throughout Arabia and United States political and military long-term relations with Saudi Arabia will be affected.

Saudi Arabia is also uniquely situated strategically in American foreign policy. The country borders on two vital waterways: the Persian Gulf and the Red Sea. In addition to being the oil pipeline of the industrial world, the Persian Gulf, as an extension of the Indian Ocean, is increasingly becoming the focus of superpower rivalry. In addition, regional powers such as Iran, Saudi Arabia, Iraq, Pakistan and India have shown noticeable interest in the gulf region. Also, the United States Navy maintains a presence in gulf waters through the small but visible Middle East force in Bahrain. More recently, the U.S. and Great Britain have discussed possible American use of air facilities on Masirah Island off the coast of Oman, practically at the entrance to the Persian Gulf.

Off Saudi Arabia's west coast, the Red Sea is another strategic waterway for the United States, Saudi Arabia and other powers. With the reopening of the Suez Canal to international navigation, the Red Sea should gain added significance for civilian as well as military navigation. Connecting the Mediterranean Sea and the Indian Ocean, the Red Sea will be used by both the American and the Russian fleets; therefore, it is logical for both American and Russian policy planners to be concerned with the conditions prevailing throughout the Red Sea basin. As a major riparian state, Saudi Arabia would logically play an important role; any long-range policy planning for a secure Red Sea basin must take the Saudi factor into consideration.

The following six points constitute the basic themes of this study:

(1) For the foreseeable future Saudi Arabia will remain a cornerstone of American foreign policy in the Middle East.

(2) American-Saudi relations, if based on a clear understanding of the interests and concerns of each of the two countries, can endure in a stable manner.

(3) Future relations between the two nations must be based on new assumptions and considerations—which would emerge from an overall review of American policy in the region. Policy assumptions developed twenty years ago are outdated and potentially dangerous.

(4) If American policy planners hope to put the burgeoning American arms sales to Saudi Arabia and other Persian Gulf countries in proper perspective, it is imperative that a new feasibility study be prepared by the National Security Council.[1]

(5) Relations with Saudi Arabia are only one aspect of the United States's relations with the entire Arab world; outstanding conflicts in Palestine and elsewhere will always be reflected in American-Saudi ties.

---

[1] In discussing the future of American-Saudi relations, Walter Pincus, executive editor of the *New Republic,* urged that the Congress and the American people be informed of the nature of American commitments to Saudi Arabia. He was referring to the American-Saudi economic and security agreement and to the United States–Saudi Arabia Joint Commission established in June 1974. Walter Pincus, "The Saudi Connection," *Washington Post,* 1 May 1975.

(6) The most enduring relationships are based on institutions, not specific regimes or rulers. Individual regimes and rulers, as the assassination of King Faysal demonstrated anew, are fragile. Stability of external relations will reflect the political stability within the system itself, and political stability in Saudi Arabia, as indeed elsewhere in the region, will be the result of political reform. In the meantime, the durability of American-Saudi relations remains unpredictable.

This study focuses primarily on the foregoing aspects of the nature and significance of an American-Saudi long-term relationship. The three factors which give this relationship significance—economics, strategy and politics—are examined in three separate chapters. Also, the policy goals and options of both the United States and Saudi Arabia are treated in each of these chapters. The study concludes with recommendations for future U.S. policy toward Saudi Arabia.

1

THE ECONOMIC DIMENSION

The Land and Its People

The Kingdom of Saudi Arabia (*al-Mamlaka al-'Arabiyya al-Sa'udiyya*), still relatively unknown to most peoples in the Western world, has in the last decade become one of the richest and largest oil-producing countries in the world and a powerful force in international relations. Saudi Arabia, a desert country with an estimated area of 618,000 square miles,[1] sprawls over 80 percent of the entire Arabian peninsula. It is about one-third of the size of the continental United States. Although no accurate statistics are available, estimates of Saudi Arabia's population range from 5 to 7 million people.

Geographically, Saudi Arabia contains nine distinct regions.[2] First, the gulf coastal region stretches from Kuwait to the United Arab Emirates and consists of shallow coast, salt flats (*sabkhah*) and flat gravel plains. The second region, called the Dahna, is an 800-mile-long strip of desert arching across the west side of Arabia from the Great Nafud to the Empty Quarter. The sands of this region are reddish in color, and several species of grazing plants are found there. The Dahna is separated from the coast by the third region, a 100-mile-wide plain of hard rock known as the Sumnian plateau. Caves, shelters (*ghawar*) and stream channels cut through this plateau. The

---

[1] Other sources estimate the number of square miles to be even greater (Congressional Quarterly, *The Middle East* [Washington, D. C.: Congressional Quarterly, 1974], p. 64).

[2] Arabian American Oil Company, *Aramco Handbook: Oil and the Middle East* (Dhahran, Saudi Arabia, 1968), pp. 208-19. For a thorough geological study of Saudi Arabia, see *Geology of the Arabian Peninsula: Sedimentary Geology of Saudi Arabia* (Washington, D. C.: U.S. Government Printing Office, 1966).

Ghawar oil field, the largest in Saudi Arabia, is in the middle of this arid, barren plateau.

The escarpment area engulfing the Najd is the fourth geographic region in Saudi Arabia; the 500-mile-long Tuwayq escarpment is the largest in the region. The fifth region, a vast expanse of gravel and rock plains, extends from the Great Nafud Desert in the north to the borders of Jordan and Iraq. This area cuts across three countries and makes up a part of what is known as the Syrian Desert.

The great sand areas constitute the sixth geographic region. These desert areas encompass hundreds of thousands of square miles and include such legendary deserts as the Great Nafud in the north and the Empty Quarter in the south. Explorers such as Bertram Thomas, H. St. John, B. Philby and Wilfred Thesiger acquired lasting fame as a result of their travels through the Empty Quarter. The western mountains and the central plateau immediately to the east of these mountains are the seventh and eighth geographic regions. To the south of these two regions lie the mountains of southern Arabia which separate Saudi Arabia from the two Yemens and the Dhufari region of Oman; these mountains comprise the ninth region. These regions vary in elevation from 3,000 feet in the central plateau to more than 10,000 feet in the highest southern elevations. Dozens of towns and villages are located in the oases found here, and fertile land lies on the mountain slopes and in the valleys. It is here that the government of Saudi Arabia hopes to develop a modern agricultural sector.

The Kingdom of Saudi Arabia is divided into four administrative regions: the Eastern Province, the Central Province, the Western Province and the Southwestern Province. Table 1 illustrates the provinces, provincial capitals and principal localities in the kingdom. The Eastern, Central and Western provinces are the most important areas: the first for its oil, the second as the capital of the house of Saud and the center of the Wahhabite sect of Islam, the third for the Muslim holy places. The estimated populations of some of the larger cities are as follows: Riyadh (the royal capital, 450,000), Jidda (the administrative capital on the Red Sea, 450,000), Mecca (250,000), Medina (150,000), Ta'if (the summer capital, 100,000), al-Khubar (100,000), Dammam (100,000), Hufuf (100,000), and Haradh (100,000).[3]

The population of Saudi Arabia is mostly Arab and Muslim of the Wahhabite sect. Roughly 50 percent of the population are

[3] First National City Bank, *Saudi Arabia: A New Economic Survey* (New York, December 1974), p. 13.

Table 1

PROVINCES, PROVINCIAL CAPITALS AND PRINCIPAL
LOCALITIES IN SAUDI ARABIA

Province	Provincial Capital	Principal Towns, Villages, Oases
Eastern Province (al-Hasa)	Dammam	al-Hasa, Qatif, Hufuf, Khubar, Dhahran, Ras Tanura, 'Abqayq.
Central Province (Najd)	Riyadh (Royal capital)	'Unayza, Burayda, al-Majma'a, al-Kharj, al-Huta, al-Hariq, al-Dirayya, Sadus, Haradh.
Western Province (Hijaz)	Mecca	Medina, Khaybar, al-Musayjid, Tabuk, al-Hanakiya, Badr Hunayn, Ta'if, Khulays, Jidda, Bisha, Ranya.
Southwestern Rrovince ('Asir)	Abha	Jizan, Najran, al-Shuqayq, Mukayla, Khamis Mushayt.

Source: Author's survey.

bedouin tribesmen, 25 percent are urban dwellers and the remaining 25 percent are settled cultivators. Approximately one-third are employed in agriculture, one-third in public service and one-fourth in trade, finance, transport and services. Only 4 percent are employed in the oil industry.[4] Some available statistics indicate that during the last decade about 25 percent of the population lived in cities with a population of over 20,000 people, 25 percent in towns of 1,000 to 19,999, and the remaining 50 percent lived in villages and tent encampments of less than 1,000.[5]

The Current State of the Economy

It is generally assumed that Saudi Arabia's economy is totally underdeveloped and that, aside from its oil industry, no economic development of any significance exists. The most cursory examination of economic activity in Saudi Arabia since the early 1960s proves this to be an unfounded assumption. As an example, more Saudis are

[4] Edmund Asfour, "Saudi Arabia," in Michael Adams, ed., *The Middle East: A Handbook* (New York: Praeger, 1971), pp. 271-81, and *The Middle East and North Africa: 1974-1975* (London: Europa Publications Limited, 1974), pp. 587-608.
[5] Ramon Knauerhase, "Saudi Arabia's Economy at the Beginning of the 1970s," *Middle East Journal*, Spring 1974, p. 127.

employed in industry, agriculture, transportation and construction than they are in the oil industry. Budgetary allocations to developmental projects in the past decade have continually increased in proportion to the national budget. The gross national product has grown annually, and real income has also increased.

Yet it must be stressed that in spite of these real strides in economic development and in spite of the accumulation of oil revenues, the Saudi economy is still far from advanced. Saudi Arabia is still technically classified as a less developed country (LDC). Oil remains the lifeline of the country, providing over 95 percent of the total national revenues.

The basic thesis of this chapter can be summarized in the following four points:

(1) The Saudi economy is expanding rapidly.

(2) Because of the lack of trained Saudi personnel and technology, Saudi Arabia will be forced to rely heavily on imported technology and advice for its economic development.

(3) Common ground for cooperation between Saudi Arabia and the United States can be found whereby Saudi economic development would be assisted, perhaps for several years, by American technology.

(4) To conclude and implement American-Saudi agreements in the economic sphere, it is essential that Saudi Arabia and the United States establish a long-term working relationship in the political sphere. This means that functional economic relationships must be preceded by open political understandings.

The establishment in June 1974 of the United States–Saudi Arabia Joint Commission on Economic Cooperation highlights the fact that common ground for cooperation does indeed exist between the two countries. It is obvious, however, that were it not for the staggering Saudi oil reserves and oil revenues, relations between Saudi Arabia and the United States would hardly be of significance. Since oil is the underpinning of the increasingly prominent Saudi posture on the world scene, this chapter concentrates on this one commodity. In addition to examining the economic map of Saudi Arabia (demography and manpower), attention is given to the long-range interests and policy goals of both the United States and Saudi Arabia. The future of economic relations between the two countries will definitely be influenced by the goals which each country sets for itself and by the policy options it elects to pursue.

Oil: Background and Prospects

Oil dominates the economic life of Saudi Arabia. As of 1 January 1975 Saudi oil reserves were put at 164.5 billion barrels, 27 percent of the total reserves of the non-Communist world.[6] In 1974 Saudi Arabia's daily production of crude oil was approximately 8.8 million barrels. The total Arab world's proven oil reserves of 376.5 billion barrels constitute over 60 percent of the total reserves of the non-Communist world, and daily production of the Arab countries during 1974 was estimated at 19 million barrels, nearly 42 percent of the total daily production of the non-Communist world.[7]

In contrast, the United States possesses no more than 6 percent of the world's proven oil reserves, and although American oil production in 1974 averaged 12 million barrels a day, the United States daily consumes 16.4 million barrels.[8] American oil imports have accordingly increased, and American dependence on Saudi oil has become a primary factor in American-Saudi relations. Table 2 indicates the regional sources of American oil imports and gives the percentage of imports and percentage of demand for each region.

Oil revenues (approximately 95 percent of total national revenues) have fueled Saudi Arabia's economic development programs and have impelled the current transition from a traditional tribal and feudal economy into a modern industrial nation. Three factors have been responsible for maintaining Saudi Arabia's oil revenues at a high level: an increase in oil production, a rise in the price of oil, and the participation agreements which led to expanded government ownership of the oil industry. Total Saudi ownership of the industry, which for the past generation has been under Aramco, is expected in the near future. Table 3 graphically illustrates the steady increase in oil production and revenues in Saudi Arabia between 1965 and 1972. Oil revenues doubled in 1973 to over $5.5 billion and nearly quadrupled in 1974 to approximately $19.4 billion. It has been estimated that by 1980 Saudi Arabia's revenues from oil will total some $36 to $50 billion, 25 percent of total estimated Organization of Oil Producing and Exporting Countries (OPEC) revenues.[9] Even by the end of 1973 Saudi Arabia's monetary reserves totaled over $4 billion.

[6] *Oil and Gas Journal*, 30 December 1974, p. 108.

[7] Ibid., pp. 108-9. For this purpose the Arab world includes Algeria, Bahrain, Egypt, Iraq, Kuwait, Libya, Kuwaiti-Saudi Neutral Zone, Oman, Qatar, United Arab Emirates and Saudi Arabia.

[8] Congressional Quarterly, *The Middle East*, p. 28.

[9] Ibid., p. 34.

Table 2

REGIONAL SOURCES OF DIRECT U.S. OIL IMPORTS

(in 1,000 barrels per day)

Direct Source	June–October 1974	Percent of Imports	Percent of Demand	June–October 1973	Percent of Imports	Percent of Demand
Arab countries	1,356.3	20.3	8.2	1,310.6	19.0	7.8
Other Eastern Hemisphere	2,194.1	32.9	13.3	1,655.7	24.0	9.8
Canada	906.3	13.6	5.5	1,285.8	18.7	7.6
Other Western Hemisphere	2,218.3	33.2	13.5	2,640.4	38.3	15.6
Total imports	6,674.8	100.0	40.5	6,892.5	100.0	40.8
Total demand	16,483.0	—	—	16,873.0	—	—

Source: *Petroleum Intelligence Weekly*, 30 December 1974, p. 5.

Table 3

ANNUAL CRUDE OIL PRODUCTION
AND OIL REVENUES IN SAUDI ARABIA

Year	Million Barrels	Million Dollars
1965	804.8	662.6
1966	950.0	789.7
1967	1,023.8	909.1
1968	1,114.0	926.8
1969	1,173.9	949.0
1970	1,386.3	1,149.7
1971	1,740.8	1,944.9
1972	2,201.8	2,779.3

Source: Saudi Arabian Monetary Agency, *Statistical Abstract* (Jidda, Saudi Arabia, December 1972), pp. 52-53 [Arabic].

Historically, the story of oil in Saudi Arabia started in the early 1930s when Aramco first began its explorations in the desert of eastern Arabia. Aramco is a unique consortium of four major American oil companies: Socal, Texaco, Exxon and Mobil. Through oil, Aramco has been a prime mover in the building of modern Saudi Arabia; the company and the kingdom have been two interlocking gears in the machinery of modernization.[10]

The first concession agreement between Standard Oil of California and Saudi Arabia was signed on 29 May 1933 and became effective on 14 July 1933. The company was officially known as the California Arabian Standard Oil Company. Eleven years later, on 31 January 1944, the name was changed to the Arabian American Oil Company (Aramco). The initial agreement established a concession for sixty-six years, from 1933 to 1999; recent participation agreements have obviously nullified the original concession.

Although Arabian oil was first produced commercially in 1938, the war years kept production at a relatively low level. Production on a large scale began in 1945, with over 50,000 barrels a day. By 1950 production had increased almost 1,000 percent to over half a million barrels a day. Table 4 shows that Aramco's daily production of crude oil hit the million mark in 1958, 2 million in 1965, and

[10] For an interesting review of the story of Aramco, see *Aramco Handbook*, pp. 107-35. Texaco joined Socal in 1936, Exxon in 1948, and Mobil Oil in 1948.

Table 4

ARAMCO CRUDE OIL PRODUCTION

Year	Barrels Daily	Total Barrels
1973	7,334,647	2,677,146,337
1972	5,733,395	2,098,422,603
1971	4,497,576	1,641,615,332
1970	3,548,865	1,295,335,759
1969	2,992,662	1,092,321,543
1968	2,829,982	1,035,773,333
1967	2,597,563	948,110,468
1966	2,392,737	873,349,148
1965	2,024,870	739,077,565
1960	1,247,140	456,453,173
1958	1,015,029	370,485,754
1950	546,703	199,546,638
1949	476,736	174,008,629
1948	390,309	142,852,989
1947	246,169	89,851,646
1945	58,386	21,310,996
1938	1,357	495,135

Source: Adapted from First National City Bank, *Saudi Arabia* (New York, December 1974), p. 11.

4 million in 1971. By the end of 1974 oil was being pumped at the rate of 8.5 million barrels a day. The cutback in production in late 1973 and early 1974 was a political decision made to protest American support of Israel in the October War. The production cuts announced in early 1975 were an economic action on the part of Saudi Arabia and other oil-producing countries to keep the price of oil at a desired level. In the spring of 1975, however, the government of Saudi Arabia announced its support for a price cut. In terms of its reserves, Saudi Arabia is capable of producing up to 20 million barrels a day by 1980.

In the early years of production Aramco paid the Saudi government a small share of the earnings; the payment had gradually risen to 50 percent of total company revenues by 1950. With the formation of OPEC in the early 1960s, Saudi Arabia, like other oil-producing countries, began to demand a larger share of the earnings, including an increase in the posted price. In the early 1970s Saudi Arabia initiated moves to participate in the ownership of Aramco. The first major participation agreement that went into effect gave Saudi Arabia 25 percent ownership of Aramco; the government's share rose to 60 percent in 1974. In the spring of 1975, the government and Aramco began discussions on the complete Saudi ownership of the company. It is expected that Aramco's role under this arrangement would be restricted to management, operations, and perhaps marketing. Oil policy decisions would be made by Saudi policy makers—a sure sign of a passing era and the dawning of a new one.

Statistics indicate that oil production has increased annually regardless of Arab and/or regional conflicts. For example, in spite of Saudi Arabia's traditional Arab position on the Palestine question, it had, prior to 1973, kept oil and politics apart. The three Arab-Israeli wars of 1947–48, 1956, and 1967 did not adversely influence the volume of production in Saudi Arabia. The closing of the Suez Canal in 1956 and the Six-Day War of 1967 did affect production, but the adverse effect was short-lived. Oil production continued to increase.

The 1973 October War sparked a new development in the world of oil. For the first time, oil was used as a political weapon; an oil embargo was declared in October 1973 by the Arab members of OPEC against the United States, Holland, and other countries. This embargo was an economic means used by the Arab oil producers for a political end: to effectuate a shift in American-Israeli relations. Saudi Arabia, the principal force behind the embargo, advocated a negotiated settlement between Israel and the "confrontation" Arab states based on Israeli withdrawal from the occupied territories. In the Saudi view, the United States was the only state capable of exerting political influence over Israel. This view was vindicated to the extent that the United States initiated and supported disengagement agreements between Israel and Egypt and between Israel and Syria in early 1974.

The embargo was also accompanied by a sharp rise in the price of oil. From January 1973 to late 1974 the price of oil quadrupled, rising from approximately $2.50 a barrel to approximately $11.00 a barrel. Saudi Arabia began to amass unprecedented revenues; the oil companies revealed unprecedented windfall profits; and the oil-consuming countries announced unprecedented balance-of-trade deficits. Economic gloom settled over the industrial world. As is shown later in this chapter, the United States, as the leading oil-consuming nation, embarked on a complicated and often confused course of energy diplomacy. Yet no substantial changes have occurred in international energy relations during the past two years as a result of this American diplomatic maneuvering. Within Saudi Arabia itself, these oil revenues have funded major economic projects in agriculture and industry. Saudi officials believe that these projects will lay the foundations of an industrially diversified country.

Economic Development and Planning

Saudi Arabia relies on its oil revenues to diversify its economy, to build a broad industrial base, and to educate and train its nationals. Through its economic diversification and manpower training programs the kingdom hopes to transform itself from a semi-theocratic monarchy into a modern industrial state. Economic planning is relatively recent, however, and many factors—social, political, and cultural—will undoubtedly impede the pace of economic growth.

Effective economic planning and industrial development began with the creation of the General Petroleum and Minerals Organization (Petromin) in 1962. Petromin was designed as an independent government agency to administer and coordinate petroleum and mineral projects, to import mineral needs, and to conduct studies on every aspect of petroleum and minerals operations.[11] Petromin's diversified approach to industrial and agricultural development can be seen in the numerous projects which have come into being since 1962. Three of the major projects that Petromin initiated have already started production. A $7 million steel-rolling mill at Jidda began production in 1968, with an annual capacity of 45,000 tons of bars and steel sheet. Another Petromin project is the Jidda oil refinery, which also started production in 1968, with an initial capacity of 12,000 barrels per day. And the $40 million Saudi Arabian Fertilizer Company (SAFCO) became operative in 1969.[12]

During the 1960s other urgent economic goals were to create a network of transportation and communications facilities, to raise the gross national product, and to expand educational opportunities. In short, from 1962 to 1970 the Saudi government and Petromin laid the foundations for the economic takeoff stage. Oil revenues, the country's gross national product, and budgetary expenditures all rose during that period. As an indication of this growth, between 1961–62

[11] Industrial Studies and Development Center, *Guide to Industrial Investment in Saudi Arabia*, 4th ed. (Riyadh, Saudi Arabia, 1974), p. 52.

[12] Saudi Arabian Monetary Agency, *Annual Report, 1970-1971*, pp. 62-65.

14

and 1971–72 the per capita income rose from 1,853 Saudi riyals to 5,189 riyals ($1 equals approximately 4 Saudi riyals). The number of children in elementary schools jumped from 199,683 boys and 57,082 girls in 1965–66 to 291,432 boys and 132,349 girls in 1970–71. In higher education during this same period the number of students more than doubled, from 3,256 men and 119 women to 7,801 men and 691 women.[13] Health services also showed marked growth. There were forty-six hospitals in 1965 and fifty in 1971. Hospital beds increased in number from 5,100 to 7,260 during this period, and the number of health clinics nearly tripled from 122 to 334.[14]

Power production, always a harbinger of industrialization, also rose significantly in this ten-year period. For the cities of Jidda, Riyadh, Mecca, Ta'if, Dhahran, and Medina, power production rose from 352.9 million kilowatt hours in 1966 to 762.9 million kilowatt hours in 1971. The highway system was also expanded greatly, thereby further strengthening the country's lines of communication. In 1961 only 2,054 kilometers (1 mile = 1.6 kilometers) of paved roads existed, but by the end of 1971 there were 8,759 kilometers of paved roads.[15]

The country's gross national product and import/export trade also showed healthy growth in the 1960s. The GNP rose from 9,109.7 million riyals in 1965–66 to 14,052.1 million riyals in 1970–71.[16] Between 1965 and 1970 exports rose from 6,838.4 million riyals to 10,907.2 million riyals, and imports rose from 2,058.4 million riyals to 3,197.2 million riyals.[17]

During the period of the first economic development plan of 1970–75, Saudi Arabia can be said to have reached the takeoff stage in practically every sector of the economy. Table 5 vividly illustrates Saudi Arabia's increasing development expenditures. Another important facet of this first plan was the emphasis placed on agricultural development. There were four major projects: a 30,000-acre irrigation project at al-Hasa in the Eastern Province, a major land reclamation and irrigation project to settle 10,000 bedouins (the Faysal Model Settlement), a dam at Wadi Jizan (which on completion will irrigate 20,000 acres), and another dam at al-Abha in the 'Asir region. A major desalination project was begun in 1973, and by the

---

[13] Ibid., p. 69.

[14] Ibid., p. 72.

[15] Ibid., p. 51.

[16] Ibid., pp. 120-21.

[17] Ibid., p. 107. Beginning with 1968, Saudi foreign trade statistics began to be listed according to the Gregorian calendar, not the Muslim calendar.

Table 5

DEVELOPMENT EXPENDITURES IN SAUDI ARABIA

(million riyals)

Ministry	1970–71	1971–72	1972–73	1973–74	1974–75
Communication	523.6	1,333.7	1,246.1	2,051.7	4,212.1
Civil Aviation	79.9	127.3	223.9	466.8	1,150.8
Agriculture & Water Resources	230.1	456.0	572.5	855.0	249.7
Petroleum & Mineral Resources	39.6	82.3	86.7	136.3	164.3
Commerce & Industry	9.2	28.9	29.9	46.0	114.4
Labor & Social Affairs	8.2	24.1	26.4	36.4	165.7
Education & Educational Institutions	24.9	125.9	255.1	565.5	1,265.6
Health	10.9	29.9	45.4	84.2	435.1
Interior (municipalities)	190.1	438.8	640.5	1,575.3	3,683.8
Hajj & Awqaf	9.4	28.2	45.7	57.5	103.8
Information	28.2	48.8	82.2	158.5	205.3
Others	1,441.9	2,312.5	3,463.2	8,229.8	14,646.4
Total	2,596.0	5,035.7	6,717.6	14,263.0	26,397.0

Source: Saudi Arabian Monetary Agency, *Statistical Summary, 1974/75* (Jidda, Saudi Arabia, 1975), p. 52.

end of 1974 the Saudi government was operating five seawater desalination plants with a total daily capacity of 12.7 million gallons.[18]

Other projects undertaken in the first economic development plan include the Petromin Lubricating Oil Company in Jidda with an annual production of 75,000 barrels, a sulfuric acid plant in Dammam, expansion of the Jidda oil refinery to a 45,000-barrels-per-day capacity, construction of a 15,000-barrels-per-day refinery in the Riyadh area, expansion of the Jidda steel-rolling mill to 100,000-tons-per-year

---

[18] Ibid., pp. 55-61.

capacity, and a long-term program for the exploitation of mineral resources.[19]

The government operates on the balanced-budget principle, and in previous years the annual budget has always been fully expended. It is worth noting at this point that in 1973–74, for the first time, the budget of 22,810 million riyals could not be expended. This was in spite of the fact that over 62 percent of the budget was allotted to developmental projects. Of the 1974–75 budget of 94,247 million riyals, less than 50 percent was expected to be spent.[20]

The $10 billion first economic development plan had scarcely come to an end in 1975 when Saudi Arabia's new king, Khalid ibn 'Abd al-'Aziz al-Saud, announced a $100 billion second economic development plan. The plan covers a five-year span from 1976 to 1980, and it is the most ambitious in the history of Saudi Arabia, calling for the expenditure of $100 billion by 1980 on all types of industrial and agricultural projects. The execution of this plan is expected to require no less than 500,000 expatriate laborers, technicians, experts, specialists, and medical doctors.[21]

Although the second development plan was prepared under the late King Faysal, King Khalid approved it within a short time after ascending the throne. Khalid was at some pains to emphasize that he intended to carry out the economic policies of his slain brother.[22] Therefore the country will most probably continue on the path of economic modernization for the foreseeable future.

Despite Saudi Arabia's creditable economic progress since 1962, several serious disabilities still hinder rapid modernization. The most pressing problem is the shortage of adequately trained manpower for all the projects envisioned under the new developmental plan. Even though accurate statistics are difficult to obtain, it is estimated that no more than 10 percent of the entire Saudi labor force, probably close to 1 million people, have completed their primary education.[23] Functional literacy is estimated to be found in only 10 to 15 percent of the population.[24] The modern educational system in the country is fifty years old; however, only a relatively small number of Saudis have benefited from it. The Ministry of Education was established in the

---

[19] *Middle East and North Africa: 1974-1975*, p. 598.

[20] Ibid.

[21] See *Washington Post*, 13 April 1975, and *al-Adwa'* (Bahrain), 24 April 1975.

[22] *al-Adwa'*, 10 April 1975.

[23] Knauerhase, "Saudi Arabia's Economy," p. 128.

[24] U.S. Department of State, *Issues: World Data Handbook* (Washington, D. C.: U.S. Government Printing Office, 1972), pp. 8-9.

1950s, but as in other sectors of Saudi society, educational expansion in terms of curriculum, facilities, students, faculties, and institutions of higher learning is a comparatively recent development. Expansion of the educational system was pushed during the 1960s and has barely begun to produce results.[25]

This lack of adequately educated and trained manpower has given rise to three potentially serious situations: (1) Many civil service positions have remained unfilled. (2) Approximately 50 to 75 percent of the positions requiring advanced degrees and/or training are being staffed by non-Saudis. (3) Many Saudis are unable to enter the work force due to a lack of training in employable skills.[26]

In addition to the critical shortage of trained Saudi manpower, economic development has been hindered in varying degrees by a number of social and psychological constraints which can only be eliminated by the passage of time. One psychological constraint is, oddly enough, the euphoria of plenty. Because of the abundant oil revenues, state-subsidized social services, and the many opportunities available to Saudi nationals with even a minimum education, many Saudis no longer perceive any urgent need for advanced training on their part. This new ethic of plenty means to many Saudis that "anything can be bought . . . the missile defense system as well as garbage collection."[27]

This ethic of plenty and the national complacency it has engendered are unique phenomena in a developing country. It certainly is deserving of further study by social scientists, but current data indicate that this attitude has drastically slowed the process of creating a reservoir of highly trained human resources in Saudi Arabia.

A strong social constraint to development has been the pervading conservative influence of the Wahhabites in the country. This can be seen most clearly in the emphasis on religious training in the educational curricula and in the nearly total exclusion of Saudi women from the work force. Opposition of the powerful religious leaders ('ulama) to many aspects of modernization has slowed the entire process. Nevertheless, with the expanding wealth, power, and influence of the central government, the king, as the chief *imam* and decision maker in the country, has been able to push through selected projects. The dependence of the 'ulama on the monarch for financial

[25] For a thorough analysis of the educational system in Saudi Arabia prior to 1965, see *Area Handbook for Saudi Arabia* (Washington, D. C.: U.S. Government Printing Office, 1966), pp. 91-104.

[26] Knauerhase, "Saudi Arabia's Economy," p. 128.

[27] Ibid., p. 139.

subsidies has resulted in an increase in the actual authority of the monarch, with a corresponding decrease in 'ulama participation in deciding the country's socioeconomic future. All of these factors must be weighed by the Saudi government as it considers policy goals and the means which it has of achieving them.

Goals and Options: Saudi Arabia

In April 1975 the Saudi government adopted a second five-year development plan for the period 1976–80. This $100 billion plan, prepared by the Central Planning Organization, is designed to transform Saudi Arabia from a one-crop economy into a modern industrial state. At the heart of this transformation lies economic diversification, which has also been the primary goal of economic planning and development since 1962.[28] Like the first five-year plan, the goals of the new plan include: (1) More rapid economic growth, (2) development of human resources, and (3) diversification of the economy to lessen dependence on oil.[29]

Economic planning and diversification have been carried out by four national, semiautonomous departments which were established for this purpose. The Saudi Arabian Monetary Agency (SAMA), created in 1952, has the sole and chief responsibility of overseeing all aspects of the central government's banking. Although SAMA's initial function was to guard the stability of the Saudi riyal, most recently it has become responsible for handling the influx of oil revenues, primarily by investing unspent money and managing the flow of revenues.

Petromin was created in 1962 as an autonomous body within the Ministry of Petroleum and Mineral Resources. Petromin was charged with developing the country's natural resources and with using these resources for national industrial development. Since 1962 Petromin has been involved with domestic as well as foreign investors in all aspects of the oil industry, from exploration to fertilizers; it is also the only domestic marketing agent for oil products. Petromin operates at least four diverse operations: geological surveying, drilling, marine petroleum construction, and tanker shipping. It is also involved in mineral exploration, refining of oil and lubricants, and the manufacture of petrochemicals and fertilizers.[30] Petromin's role in pro-

[28] *Washington Post*, 13 April 1975.
[29] First National City Bank, *Saudi Arabia*, p. 22.
[30] Ibid., p. 24.

moting oil-related industrialization is likely to expand during the second economic development plan.

The third agent of economic development is the Central Planning Organization (CPO), a government agency created in 1965. The CPO is responsible for the preparation of national development plans and for the general course of economic progress in the country. The CPO is staffed by Saudi and foreign professionals, including some full-time American specialists from the Stanford Research Institute.[31] The CPO, with the assistance of the Stanford Research Institute, was responsible for the preparation of the first and second five-year plans.

The fourth development agency, the Industrial Studies and Development Center (ISDC), was formed in 1967 under the auspices of the United Nations Development Programme (UNDP).[32] The ISDC is charged with preparing feasibility studies on individual industrial projects, and it is composed of high-ranking bureaucrats from government departments and agencies that are involved in industry. Although the ISDC does not participate in policy planning concerning economic development, it is a serious contributor to the nation's overall economic development. Through the advice it offers to government agencies and the assistance it renders to private enterprise, the ISDC performs a unique role in solving the country's technical problems.

In order to realize the three objectives of economic growth, development of human resources and economic diversification, the first five-year plan called for government expenditures of $10 billion. The areas affected were education, public health, transportation, communications, agriculture and water resources, and defense. This plan was the first major attempt on the part of the Saudi government to utilize oil revenues for national development on a large scale and on a definitely scientific basis. The plan was also the first deliberate attempt by the Saudi government to actually begin the process of building a modern state, beginning with the most essential infrastructure.

Aside from the expenditures specified in the first plan, the government had planned to invest surplus revenues in the oil industry, primarily as downstream investment. An indication of this official policy was first made in a speech by the minister of oil and mineral resources, Sheikh Ahmad Zaki Yamani, in Washington in the fall of 1972. In that speech Sheikh Yamani called for a commercial oil agreement between Saudi Arabia and the United States based on the

---

[31] Ibid., p. 23.
[32] Ibid.

principle of participation. Saudi Arabia would, according to Yamani, guarantee the United States a continuous flow of oil, and in return Saudi Arabia would participate in the marketing of oil from the well to the gas pump.[33]

Nevertheless, the world energy crisis of 1973 and 1974, the rising prices of oil, the accumulation of petrodollars and the sobering realization that oil is a finite natural resource have led the Saudi government to change its investment philosophy from downstream back to the kingdom.[34] Determined to diversify its economy and to prepare Saudi Arabia for the post-oil era, the government brought forth the second five-year plan, an ambitious undertaking which will pour into the country more funds than can possibly be spent. Of the $28 billion 1974–75 budget, the Saudi government actually expects to spend only $13 billion, or 46 percent.[35] Because of this limited absorptive capacity, huge surpluses of petrodollars are expected to accumulate in the country.

Economic development and modernization mean in essence that Saudi policy planners must work toward the "transformation of the social and institutional environment in such a way as to make possible the formation and expansion, on a sustained basis, of a managerial and skilled elite and a labour force that can assimilate, adapt, modify and apply modern science and technology." [36] In order for Saudi Arabia to proceed with building a modern state according to the second five-year plan at least five conditions must prevail:

(1) a stable market for Saudi oil at sufficiently high prices to guarantee sufficient revenues for the plan,

(2) stable international trade and shipping operations,

(3) an atmosphere of cooperation between the oil producers and the oil consumers,

(4) open access of Saudi Arabia to Western, particularly American, technology and expertise, and, most importantly,

---

[33] *World Energy Demands and the Middle East* (Washington, D. C.: The Middle East Institute, 1972), p. 99, part 1. The full text of Sheikh Yamani's speech is on pp. 95-100.

[34] First National City Bank, *Saudi Arabia*, p. 25.

[35] Ibid.

[36] This was one of three basic prerequisites developed in a United Nations study on the successful application of scientific and technological knowledge to development in the Middle East. The other two prerequisites were a science-based industry and a science-based agriculture. See United Nations Economic and Social Office in Beirut, *Regional Plan of Action for the Application of Science and Technology to Development in the Middle East* (New York: United Nations Publications, 1974), p. 4.

(5) Saudi Arabian policy makers must always realize that their new-found riches are only useful in an atmosphere of international cooperation.

The inflationary aspects of the international economic malaise during 1973 and 1974 could create problems for Saudi Arabia in the long run, unless an international system of indexing is established. Inflation in the industrial world affects the oil-producing countries as well, and since Saudi Arabia imports practically all of its needs, from foodstuffs to heavy machinery, a troubled economy internationally will ultimately lead to economic dislocation in Saudi Arabia, which in turn will retard the process of economic development. Likewise, since Saudi Arabia lacks the native manpower and technology to proceed with its own economic development effectively, it must import both. Therefore cooperation between Saudi Arabia and the oil consumers, especially those countries that are likely sources of technology and manpower, such as the United States, can result in a healthy economic exchange. If such an exchange can be developed, the world's economy will benefit. Sheikh Ahmad Zaki Yamani stated at a special 1974 energy seminar in Washington, D. C., that Saudi policy planners recognize the need for international economic cooperation. He suggested that the United States and other industrial nations should do three things: (1) adjust themselves "to the new economic reality that there is a transfer of wealth from the industrial world to a group of developing nations, the oil-producing nations," [37] (2) sit down with the newly wealthy group of states in order to "see how you can meet their requirements and how you can solve your problem," [38] and (3) establish a committee representing the oil producers, the industrial countries, and the developing countries to jointly discuss the world's energy needs in a spirit of cooperation. Sheikh Yamani said that confrontation and newspaper headline scare tactics "will create an atmosphere of hostility, and will take us away from what we want." [39]

In summary, to achieve its economic goals the Saudi government, in cooperation with OPEC, has apparently selected the option of maximizing its profits to obtain needed revenues to fund its programs; it would also apparently wish to enter into mutually beneficial agreements with industrialized countries, especially the United States, to

---

[37] *Dialogue on World Oil: Highlights of a Conference on World Oil Problems* (Washington, D. C.: American Enterprise Institute, 1974), p. 27.

[38] Ibid.

[39] Ibid., p. 26.

obtain the expertise it needs to develop its human and mineral resources.

Goals and Options: The United States

United States interests in the Arab/Persian Gulf and in Saudi Arabia are real, diverse and complicated; they must be faced squarely by American long-range policy planners. They must also be understood by Saudi officials on not only the American-Saudi bilateral level, but also within the worldwide context of the United States as a superpower concerned about its security and as a major energy consumer concerned about its present and future needs for oil.

American long-range policy goals toward Saudi Arabia fall into three categories: economic, political, and strategic. Future policy options must be selected from within these three categories, and for the sake of rationality, intelligibility, and future effectiveness, policy goals and options must be treated as one comprehensive and all-encompassing entity. For the purposes of this study, however, the analysis of American interests in Saudi Arabia follows a twofold approach: first, each category of interests will be reviewed separately as it relates to the specific topic of discussion. Second, overall American interests will be reviewed in the conclusion.

Thus, American economic interests in Saudi Arabia can be very easily reduced to one word: oil.[40] Variations on this basic theme include the following: how can the flow of oil be guaranteed to the United States—indeed, the entire industrial world—at a reasonable price? When will a combination of restricted flow and optimum prices be considered a case of economic strangulation? Should the United States actively attempt to retrieve its petrodollars in the form of direct or indirect Saudi investment? What method of retrieval should be used? Several plans made public during the past two years have ranged from the ludicrous and simplistic to the most serious and intricate. Washington has probably considered the possible use of force and price fixing in the form of open commercial treaties. Amidst all this planning one thing should remain clear: whatever course of action American policy makers will finally adopt from whatever policy option, it will definitely involve and be of concern to all Arab countries and to the entire OPEC group. Repercussions from American energy policies will be felt throughout the world.

---

[40] For an examination of American economic interests in the Arab/Persian Gulf, see Emile A. Nakhleh, *Arab-American Relations in the Persian Gulf* (Washington, D. C.: American Enterprise Institute, 1975), pp. 66-67.

It is the contention of this author that American long-range interests can be best served by cooperation with Saudi Arabia. Confrontation will not serve American interests, secure more oil, or reduce the price of oil. American oil policy must focus on one simple question: how to guarantee the flow of Saudi oil at reasonable prices. In examining this most basic policy question, the following analysis concentrates on American-Saudi commercial agreements, such as Saudi investments in the United States, imports and exports, and special bilateral relations.

American economic policy toward Saudi Arabia has been significantly influenced by the October 1973 oil embargo and its aftermath. Although the embargo ended in the spring of 1974, five months after it began, American policy still suffers from the embargo psychology. American-Saudi economic relations throughout 1974 and 1975 have exhibited characteristics which often seem contradictory, depending on whether these relations are reviewed by Congress or by the President. The most immediate policy concern in early 1974 was to end the oil embargo against the United States. Since the late King Faysal had cited the Arab-Israeli conflict and the United States's staunch support of Israel as the immediate causes of the embargo, the American government, in the person of Secretary of State Henry Kissinger, used its good offices actively in a novel form of shuttle diplomacy to conclude disengagement agreements between Israel and Egypt and between Israel and Syria. The oil embargo was accordingly lifted in March 1974. Following the withdrawal of the embargo, the United States forthwith embarked on an intensive search for a long-range energy policy. Two overall themes were stressed: the need for American energy independence and the call for international economic cooperation.

Project Independence, announced by former President Richard M. Nixon in November 1973, became the operative program for domestic energy independence. It was an ambitious goal, and it has to date proved somewhat elusive.[41] On another front, President Ford's address at the United Nations General Assembly on 18 September 1974 established the theoretical foundation for global economic interdependence and cooperation. In his United Nations address, President Ford linked production and the cost of energy to the level

---

[41] In calling for self-sufficiency in energy by 1980, former President Nixon presented Project Independence in the following statement: "Let us set as our national goal, in the spirit of Apollo, with the determination of the Manhattan Project, that by the end of this decade we will have developed the potential to meet our own energy needs without depending on any foreign energy sources." Congressional Quarterly, *The Middle East*, p. 27.

of economic development throughout the world. Global cooperation was seen as the only viable future approach if human survival was to be guaranteed. The President stressed four principles in his speech: "All nations must substantially increase production. . . . All nations must seek to achieve a level of prices which not only provides an incentive to producers but which consumers can afford. . . . All nations must avoid the abuse of man's fundamental needs for the sake of narrow or national bloc advantages. . . . The nations of the world must assure that the poorest among us are not overwhelmed by rising prices of the imports necessary for their survival." [42]

The note of cooperation was again sounded by Secretary of State Kissinger in Chicago in 1974. Kissinger called on the consumer nations to present a unified front in the face of what he called the "profound challenge to our courage, our vision, and our will." [43] Kissinger's strategy for action in that speech included domestic energy conservation, the search for alternative energy sources, the safeguarding of international economic security, and cooperation among the oil-consuming nations.[44] The concerted efforts of the United States government in regard to oil in 1974–75 have been aimed at forcing a reduction in the price of oil, breaking the back of OPEC, and luring petrodollars from the oil countries back to the United States.

In its attempt to attract Saudi petrodollars, the American government has made a conscious effort to encourage trade with Saudi Arabia, especially in the form of exports of American goods and by inducing the Saudi government to invest in the United States, either in government securities and bonds or in the private sector. Although American exports to Saudi Arabia have not risen as dramatically as those of countries such as Japan or France, they have shown a definite increase over the past several years and are continuing to rise. Yet, because of certain negative political attitudes and other political and economic considerations on the part of gulf governments toward the United States, "Buy American" has met with some resistance.[45]

---

[42] See the text of the President's speech in the *Washington Post*, 19 September 1974.

[43] "Energy Crisis: Strategy for Cooperative Action," a speech by the Secretary of State (Washington, D. C.: Department of State, Bureau of Public Affairs, 14 November 1974), p. 1.

[44] Ibid., p. 4.

[45] See a statement on the "U.S. Persian Gulf Policy" by Congressman Lee H. Hamilton, chairman of the Subcommittee on the Near East and South Asia in the *Congressional Record*. U.S. Congress, House of Representatives, Committee on Foreign Affairs, *The Persian Gulf, 1974: Money, Politics, Arms, and Power* (Washington, D. C.: U.S. Government Printing Office, 1975), pp. 262-67.

Table 6

U.S. EXPORTS TO SAUDI ARABIA BY MAJOR CATEGORY, 1971–MAY 1974

Category	1971	1972	1973	1974 (January–May)
Food and live animals	$ 22,263,029	$ 32,011,815	$ 63,865,761	$ 42,171,588
Beverages and tobacco	7,220,714	10,778,159	12,626,768	6,689,110
Crude materials, inedible, except fuel	866,975	1,598,958	3,591,365	2,236,079
Minerals, fuels, lubes	2,544,364	4,812,769	4,042,627	1,973,142
Oils & fats (animal & vegetable)	1,211,220	597,703	1,274,205	866,879
Chemicals	9,923,292	11,565,762	16,571,218	7,361,764
Manufactured goods by chief material	14,083,157	20,829,390	37,584,194	24,598,619
Machinery & transportation equipment	79,944,469	193,667,962	234,763,744	135,608,383
Miscellaneous manufactured articles, n.e.c.	7,422,225	12,291,352	17,551,190	10,454,319
Items not classified by kind	2,695,137	5,703,586	6,565,449	4,666,464
Special category [a]	15,361,139	18,383,519	41,774,684	67,867,900
Total	$163,555,721	$312,240,975	$440,211,205	$304,494,247

[a] Consists of arms, ammunition, and other military items generally under the export control jurisdiction of the Department of State.
Source: U.S. Congress, House of Representatives, Committee on Foreign Affairs, *The Persian Gulf, 1974: Money, Politics, Arms, and Power*, 93d Congress, 2d session (Washington, D. C.: U.S. Government Printing Office, 1975), p. 56.

Table 6 shows the volume of American exports to Saudi Arabia since 1971.

Encouragement of investment in United States government bonds and securities is another policy option that has been used to stimulate the "recycling" of petrodollars. During his visit to Saudi Arabia in 1974, Secretary of the Treasury William Simon encouraged the Saudis to buy twenty-, twenty-five-, and thirty-year long-term bonds. The

Figure 1

U.S.-SAUDI ARABIA JOINT COMMISSION

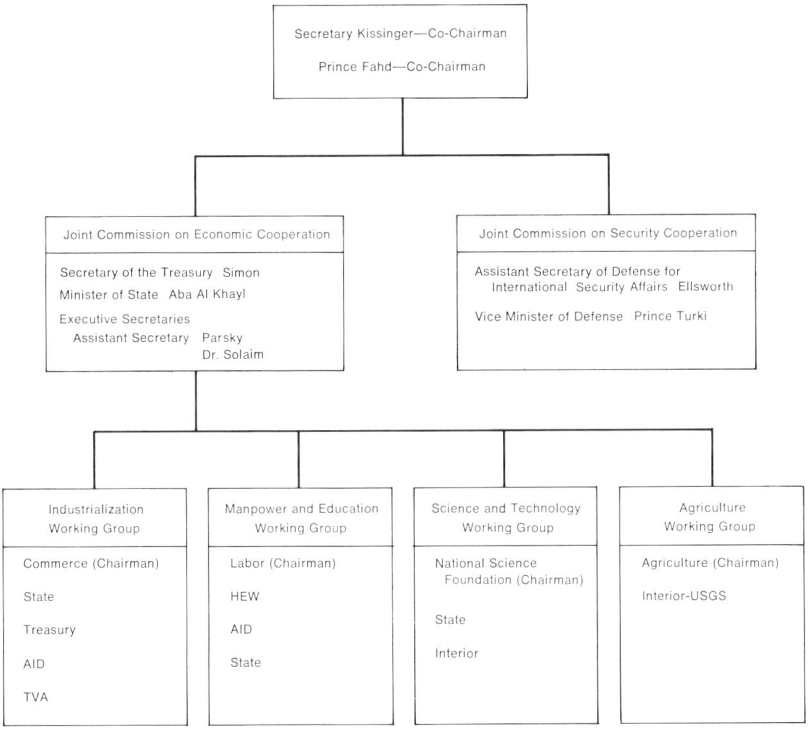

Note: The U.S.-Saudi Arabia Joint Commission was established 8 June 1974 by Secretary Kissinger and Prince Fahd. Informal meetings were held during Secretary Simon's July 1974 visit in Saudi Arabia. The Joint Commission on Economic Cooperation met in February 1975 and the Joint Commission on Security Cooperation met 10-12 November 1974. Working group meetings were held as follows: Industrialization—21-23 July 1974 and 26-28 September 1974, Manpower and Education—24-25 July 1974, Science and Technology—16-17 September 1974, and Agriculture—14-15 September 1974.

Source: U.S. Congress, House of Representatives, Committee on Foreign Affairs, *The Persian Gulf, 1974: Money, Politics, Arms, and Power,* 93rd Congress, 2d session (Washington, D. C.: U.S. Government Printing Office, 1975), p. 258.

figure he suggested to the Saudis was slightly over $6 billion.[46] By 30 November 1974 it was estimated that the holdings of American government obligations by Middle Eastern oil-producing countries were in excess of $2 billion. (On 31 December 1973, in contrast, the holdings were $81 million.) Saudi Arabia holds the lion's share of these obligations.[47]

In addition to encouraging Saudi investment in the United States, sales of American arms and other military services dramatically increased during 1974. Very complex relationships in this area exist between the United States and Saudi Arabia, and it is estimated that in fiscal 1975 Saudi orders for American arms and defense systems will be close to $1 billion. In addition, the United States government and the American defense industry have been actively engaged in massive military training programs in Saudi Arabia, ranging from the construction of missile systems to the retraining of the Saudi National Guard. Authorized exports to Saudi Arabia of defense items on the munitions list almost quadrupled between 1973 and 1974.[48]

The most ambitious cooperative program between the United States and Saudi Arabia has been the United States-Saudi Arabia Joint Commissions on Economic and Security Cooperation. The commissions were established by Secretary of State Kissinger and Crown Prince Fahd ibn 'Abd al-'Aziz al-Saud, brother of both the late King Faysal and the present King Khalid. Four working groups were also established under the Joint Commission on Economic Cooperation: Industrialization, Manpower and Education, Science and Technology, and Agriculture. Figure 1 gives a detailed picture of the two commissions and their working groups. Through these commissions the governments of Saudi Arabia and the United States "expressed their readiness to expand cooperation in the fields of economics, technology, and industry, and in the supply of the Kingdom's requirements for defensive purposes." [49]

With the above-stated official commitment to joint cooperation, it would seem foolish to contemplate such other options as the use of force. But since the use of force against the oil-producing countries has been publicly raised, it will be analyzed in the chapter on the strategic dimension of American long-range policy toward Saudi Arabia.

---

[46] Ibid., p. 141.

[47] Ibid., p. 140.

[48] See the statement of Richard R. Violette, director for sales negotiations, Defense Security Assistance Agency, before the House Subcommittee on the Near East and South Asia, 30 July 1974. Ibid., pp. 5-14.

[49] Ibid., p. 259.

2
THE POLITICAL DIMENSION

An Overview

Saudi Arabia is a conservative Muslim monarchy ruled by a powerful king whose authority derives from a large, closely knit royal family (al-Saud), an influential group of religious scholars (*'ulama*), and tribal support as expressed by the allegiance of powerful tribal chiefs (*sheikhs*) throughout the land. The constitutional basis of government is lodged in Islamic law (*shari'a*). The two primary supports of the *shari'a* are the *Sunna*, or traditions, and the *Hadith*, or the sayings and actions of the Prophet Muhammad.[1] Saudi religious conservatism and support for a strict adherence to the faith are based on the Wahhabite movement, founded by the eighteenth-century religious reformer Muhammad 'Abd al-Wahhab in the heart of the Arabian peninsula.

The Saudi royal family has assumed, by fact of geography, the role of the defender of the faith and protector of Islam's two holiest places, Mecca and Medina. Special moral significance is even attached to the Saudi monarch's utterances on Jerusalem, Islam's third holiest shrine. In addition to Saudi Arabia's special position for Muslims throughout the world, much like the Vatican for Catholics, the oil-derived wealth has added a new dimension of power and influence, far exceeding the country's size or religious stature. This power and influence has given Saudi Arabia international stature and has drawn the world's attention to the country and its institutions.

The jolting transformation from a *terra incognita* to world prominence has placed Saudi society, with all of its traditions and

---

[1] The two other sources of the *shari'a* according to the classical theory of Islam are the *'ijma'*, or consensus, and the *qiyas*, or analogy.

institutions, under scrutiny—an uncomfortable condition for any society. It is a situation which Saudi rulers cannot wish away and to which they must adjust. As a result of this international prominence, the connection between Saudi Arabia's internal political system and the country's regional and international foreign policy has come into sharp focus. There is also the pressure brought to bear by systemic social change, occasioned by the pressure new wealth and a growing middle class create.

The thesis of this chapter is therefore twofold: an organic relationship exists between Saudi Arabia's domestic politics and its foreign policy, and whatever political reforms or changes occur within Saudi society and the Saudi body politic will substantially influence the future direction of political development throughout the region, especially as it concerns the status and durability of the present regimes. Since the United States has direct economic, political and strategic interests in the region, it is necessary to reflect on the nature of the Saudi political system and its future development.

Political Infrastructures and Dynamics

The assassination of King Faysal in March 1975 and the smooth, swift succession to power by King Khalid highlighted several characteristics of the Saudi political system that have proved somewhat surprising to the outside world, neighboring and distant states alike, where the stability of the Saudi political system has of course been the subject of considerable speculation.[2]

The first characteristic is the unquestioned power which the royal family still wields in shaping state policy. Although the story of King Khalid's succession will have to wait for future historians to be told fully, it is now known that immediately following the assassination the inner council of the royal family convened in an extraordinary meeting and agreed to bestow the kingship and the premiership on Khalid. The new king, in turn, with the approval of the family, appointed Prince Fahd the first deputy prime minister and crown prince, thereby putting him in line for succession to the throne.

---

[2] Four royal communiqués were issued simultaneously on 25 March 1975, the day King Faysal was assassinated, announcing the assassination, arranging the funeral, declaring the royal family's allegiance to the new king, and detailing the assassination. The third communiqué was obviously the most significant and stated that the new king had, immediately upon assuming the kingship, received the allegiance of five of the most powerful members of the family: four brothers (Fahd, Sa'd, Nasir, and Muhammad) and an uncle ('Abdalla). See al-Adwa' (Bahrain), 27 March 1975. See also J. C. Hurewitz, "Saudi Arabia: Stability during Transition," New York Times, 30 March 1975.

King Khalid has in fact given Prince Fahd considerable authority over the internal affairs of the country. Most of these decisions were made by the royal family's inner council before the assassination was publicly announced. "Like the murder," wrote Jim Hoagland of the *Washington Post*, "the carefully orchestrated succession has been a family affair." [3]

Other marked characteristics of the royal family are loyalty, cohesiveness, and political acumen. Although the royal family numbers in the thousands, the country's actual governing in terms of wealth, power and influence rests with a handful of brothers and half-brothers of the late King Faysal, all of whom are the sons of 'Abd al-'Aziz al-Saud, the founder of modern Saudi Arabia. The most powerful of the brothers are nine: seven full brothers (the "Seven Sudeiris") whose mother, the wife of 'Abd al-'Aziz, was a member of the Sudayri tribe, and two half-brothers (King Khalid and Prince 'Abdalla) whose mother, another wife of 'Abd al-'Aziz, was a member of the Jiluwi tribe.[4]

Among themselves, the brothers in essence have charge of the entire country: Khalid as king and prime minister, Fahd as crown prince and first deputy prime minister, 'Abdalla as the head of the national guard, Nayif as interior minister and head of internal security, and Sultan as minister of defense and aviation. Two other ministerial positions, though not held by any of the brothers, are of significance: the Ministry of Foreign Affairs, headed by Prince Saud, son of the late King Faysal, and the Ministry of Petroleum and Mineral Resources, which is still headed by Sheikh Ahmad Zaki Yamani, probably the Saudi Arabian figure most familiar to the Western world.

Religious influence is yet another powerful characteristic of the Saudi socio-political system. The power of the religious leaders ('ulama) was once again demonstrated during the succession of King Khalid to the throne. A brief review of political developments in recent years shows that the 'ulama position on royal power has played a crucial role in the drama of the last two successions. During the power struggle between King Saud and Faysal in March 1964, the *grand mufti*, head of the 'ulama, issued a religious legal proclamation (*fatwa*) supporting Faysal against Saud. The *fatwa* essentially endorsed the transfer of power from Saud to Faysal, and when Faysal announced in November 1964 that he would rule in accordance with

---

[3] Jim Hoagland, "Who Rules Saudi Arabia?" *Washington Post*, 8 April 1975.

[4] "The Seven Sudeiris," *Newsweek*, 7 April 1975, p. 25. (This is a special article on King Faysal's assassination and the Saudi royal family.)

the country's Islamic tradition, the *grand mufti* pledged allegiance to him. During the events of another March, eleven years later, the *'ulama* again played a decisive role in their support of and allegiance to Khalid's accession to the throne.

Perhaps the most basic characteristic of the Saudi system is its remarkable stability—a result of consciously balanced and carefully supported tribal traditions, religious influence, family power, and, of course, oil wealth. This combination is the heart of traditional political dynamics in Saudi Arabia. In recent years, however, new factors have begun increasingly to disturb this equilibrium. Among them are: the new wealth, sprawling urban centers, the developing middle class, the growing numbers of the educated, the technocratic elite, the rapidly arming national guard with its elitist officer class, and the uniquely wealthy, foreign-educated, and potentially powerful class of royal princes. These are all new elements which have begun to challenge the country's political traditionalism. Consequently, within the next decade Saudi politics will be put under strong pressure by several emerging dichotomies: traditionalism versus modernity, tribalism versus urbanism, Islamic-Wahhabite social rigidity versus secular mobility, family autocracy versus participatory government, and customary tribal rules of conduct versus written constitutional law. The durability of the Saudi political system will be determined by the reconciliation of these dichotomies. Outcomes are not difficult to envision, and regardless of the ultimate results, the royal family must take cognizance of these new forces, powerful urges which cannot be easily contained within the traditional Saudi system of tribal and family loyalties.[5]

Modern History

The house of Saud, like other ruling families in other Arabian peninsula states, amirates, and sheikhdoms, descends from one of the tribes which had roamed the Arabian desert in centuries past. The al-Saud family, like the al-Sabah of Kuwait and the al-Khalifa of Bahrain, stems from the 'Anizah tribal federation that roamed the deserts of central Arabia. Other tribes and clans from which present ruling families in the Arabian peninsula states have descended are well illustrated in Figure 2.

Saudi Arabia's history in the eighteenth and nineteenth centuries began in 1742, when Muhammad ibn Saud, the amir of al-Dir'iyya,

---

[5] For a discussion of traditional political dynamics, see *Area Handbook for Saudi Arabia*, pp. 151-60.

Figure 2
TRIBAL MAP OF THE ARABIAN PENINSULA

Source: Arabian American Oil Company, *Aramco Handbook: Oil and the Middle East* (Dhahran, Saudi Arabia, 1968), p. 54 (with modifications).

near Riyadh in the Najd region, gave refuge to Muhammad ibn 'Abd al-Wahhab (1703–1792) and embraced the puritanical Wahhabite version of Islam. Muhammad ibn Saud and his descendants began to spread their hegemony and the Wahhabite doctrine out of the Najd into other parts of Arabia. After a series of bloody conquests, battles and tribal wars, the house of Saud established its rule throughout most of Arabia from the Persian Gulf to the Red Sea, thereby including Mecca, Medina, and the entire Hijaz region.

Throughout this period, Saudi rule and governmental organization were based on three interlocking supports: tribalism, religious authority, and Wahhabism. The ultimate political and religious authority to make decisions, however, resided in the person of the Saudi ruler. Within this autocratic rule, local government, which was essentially composed of a *qadi* (religious judge), a *mufti* (religious scholar), and a governor, operated on the basis of the Islamic *shari'a*, or customary law, and tribal tradition. This was essentially a feudal system of relationships perpetuated by the Saudi dynasty.[6] Figure 3 gives a simplified genealogical table of the Saudi kings. The Islamic tribal tradition as a basis of Saudi rule continued well into the twentieth century.

The contemporary political history of Saudi Arabia is identified with the rule of 'Abd al-'Aziz al-Saud from 1932, the year the Kingdom of Saudi Arabia was established as an independent state, until his death in 1953.[7] 'Abd al-'Aziz's rule may, in the best sense of the term, be described as one of feudal overlordship. His absolute and benevolent monarchy strove toward the institutionalization of an Islamic tribalism based on the rigid unitarian Wahhabite concept of the state. 'Abd al-'Aziz also consolidated his power through the settlement of state boundaries, the control of diverse tribes and tribal rivalries, and the accumulation of revenues, meager as they initially were, from oil concessions. The Koran was the guiding principle of the state, and tribal traditions and customs were the operative principles of the king's one-man government. In terms of the Saudi political community, 'Abd al-'Aziz succeeded in ending tribal strife and in establishing a nation-state, the largest in the peninsula.[8]

Evolution of Government Institutions

The building of modern state institutions in Saudi Arabia has come about in three formal steps. In October 1953, King 'Abd al-'Aziz issued a royal decree establishing a ministerial system and forming a Council of Ministers to act as an advisory body to the king. Although it was a significant step toward modern government, the Saudi Council of Ministers possessed no executive powers; the king continued to exercise his prerogatives as chief of state, head of the royal family, prince of the faithful (amir al-mu'minin), and head of all tribal sheikhs (shaikh al-mashayikh).[9] The transfer of the ministries from

[6] For a historical survey of the Saudi dynasty during the eighteenth and nineteenth centuries, see ibid., pp. 30-33.

[7] For a synopsis of modern Saudi history, see Ramon Knauerhase, "Saudi Arabia: A Brief History," *Current History*, February 1975, pp. 74-79, 82-83 and 88. For a specific focus on 'Abd al-'Aziz's reign, see David G. Edens, "The Anatomy of the Saudi Revolution," *International Journal of Middle East Studies*, January 1974, pp. 50-64.

[8] David G. Edens, "The Anatomy of the Saudi Revolution," p. 64.

[9] For an informative analysis of the socio-political composition of Saudi society, see Abdul H. Raoof, "The Kingdom of Saudi Arabia," in Tareq Y. Ismael, ed., *Governments and Politics of the Contemporary Middle East* (Homewood, Ill.: The Dorsey Press, 1970), pp. 353-79.

Figure 3

GENEALOGICAL TABLE OF THE HOUSE OF SAUD (SIMPLIFIED), WITH THE ORDER AND DURATION OF RULE

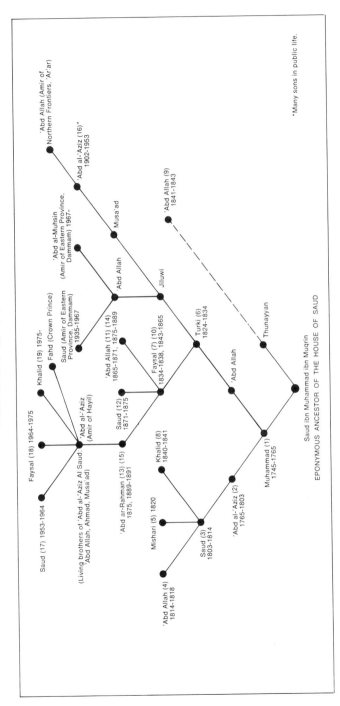

Source: Adapted from Arabian American Oil Company, *Aramco Handbook: Oil and the Middle East* (Dhahran, Saudi Arabia, 1968), p. 48.

Jidda in the Hijaz to Riyadh in the Najd in the mid-1950s signaled the complete consolidation of the authority of the house of Saud as a ruling dynasty in Arabia.[10]

The duties and functions of the Council of Ministers were defined in May 1958 by King Saud ibn 'Abd al-'Aziz.[11] According to this significant decree, the Council of Ministers was given executive and legislative duties for the first time in the history of the Saudi state. It was a definite indication that a gradual process of political modernization was taking place in the country, that a process of detribalization was occurring, that the governing of the state had become a complex responsibility which the monarch alone could no longer discharge, that Saudi Arabia was becoming a welfare state due to its increasing oil revenues, and that a central bureaucratic government organization was being created.

In accordance with Article 11 of the 1958 Statute of the Council of Ministers, the council is composed of a president (the prime minister), a vice-president (deputy prime minister), departmental ministers, ministers of state, and advisors to the king. Appointments to the Council of Ministers are made by royal decree. Article 18 of the same statute states that the Council of Ministers shall legislate in all major aspects of the state. The council was also entrusted with the execution of this policy.[12] Faysal, the king's brother, was appointed prime minister and crown prince.

This gradual evolution of Saudi Arabia into a modern state with a functioning government was boosted significantly in the social and economic spheres when, in November 1962, Prime Minister Faysal issued his ten-point program for the modernization of the country.[13] The ten-point program called for many of the basic elements of modern government:

(1) Promulgation of a "Basic Law" (or constitution) based on the *shari'a* and the Koran.

(2) Regulation of local government.

(3) Creation of a Supreme Judicial Council and a Ministry of Justice.

(4) Establishment of a Judiciary Council.

(5) New emphasis on the spread of Islam.

---

[10] *Area Handbook for Saudi Arabia*, p. 136.

[11] Abid A. al-Marayati, *Middle Eastern Constitutions and Electoral Laws* (New York: Praeger, 1958), pp. 293-313.

[12] Ibid., p. 296.

[13] Gerald DeGaury, *Faisal: King of Saudi Arabia* (London: Arthur Barker, Ltd., 1966), pp. 147-51.

(6) Reorganization of the Committee for Public Morality.

(7) Social legislation to improve the standard of living of the average Saudi citizen.

(8) Coordination of economic development programs and efforts.

(9) Establishment of priority items in the economic development plan, such as an industrialization program.

(10) Abolition of slavery.

Most of the social and economic provisions of the ten-point program have been implemented. Ambitious programs in industrialization, health, education, and welfare have been set in motion. In the political sphere, however, no constitution has been written. The king's authority has not been diminished. Nevertheless, the organizational structure has been formalized, new ministries have been created, and the central bureaucracy has grown in size. Although Figure 4 is ten years old, the government structure has not significantly changed.

The demands for political reform by Saudis are on the rise, and the recent government statement promising the promulgation of a constitution is believed to be a response to these rising demands.[14] The impetus for political reform is being generated by the rapidly expanding middle class, a new stratum of the population that is educated, semi-secular, bourgeois, and nontraditional. This new class seems destined to play a central role in the future of Saudi Arabia.

The New Middle Class and Political Reform

Whether it is called a middle class, a new middle class, or a technocratic elite, a different social stratum is developing in Saudi Arabia. Recent studies have attributed the rise of this new group to education, wealth, urban entrepreneurship, technocracy, managerial bureaucracy, and, of course, the armed services officer corps.[15] Saudi Arabia's middle class exhibits general characteristics similar to other middle classes in the Middle East, and the nature, composition, training,

---

[14] Jim Hoagland, "Saudis Announce Plans for Political Reforms," *Washington Post*, 2 April 1975. The government statement promised that a consultative council (*majlis shura*) would be formed.

[15] See William Rugh, "Emergence of a New Middle Class in Saudi Arabia," *Middle East Journal*, Winter 1973, pp. 7-20; James A. Bill, "Class Analysis and the Dialectics of Modernization in the Middle East," *International Journal of Middle East Studies*, October 1973, pp. 417-34; and Manfred W. Wenner, "Saudi Arabia: Survival of Traditional Elites," in Frank Tachau, ed., *Political Elites and Political Development in the Middle East* (Cambridge, Mass.: Schenkman Publishing Company, Inc., 1975), pp. 157-91.

Figure 4

GOVERNMENT ORGANIZATION IN SAUDI ARABIA, 1965

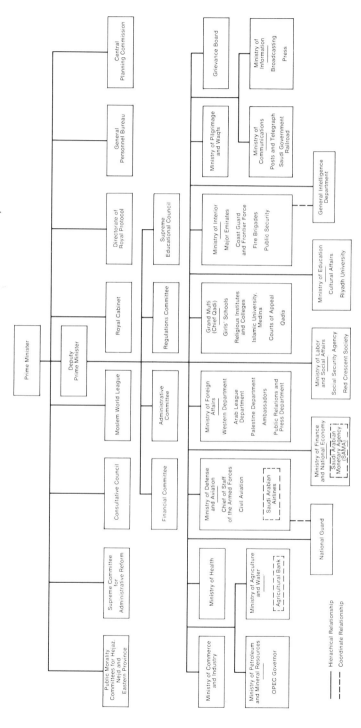

Source: *Area Handbook for Saudi Arabia* (Washington, D. C.: U.S. Government Printing Office, 1966), p. 141.

38

background, and demands of this class will have a significant impact on the future direction of Saudi Arabia as a political community. It is safe to assume that the traditionally organic nature of Saudi society and the stable relationships between the monarchy and its subjects will be affected by the influence of the middle class within the Saudi polity.

Middle Eastern societies have traditionally consisted of a small, powerful, and wealthy upper class and a large powerless class of landless, uneducated, and unskilled workers, peasants, and nomads. A very small middle class of entrepreneurs has usually managed to exist somewhere between these two extremes of the social spectrum. Saudi Arabia is no exception.

The Saudi upper class has always included the royal family, tribal sheikhs, the *'ulama*, the *shari'a* judges, and the country's wealthier merchant families. This class has ruled the country, has benefited economically from the system, and has had a definite interest in maintaining the Saudi family-controlled and family-directed status quo. In the modern history of Saudi Arabia, the elite has acted as an extension of the house of Saud.[16] It has perceived its legitimacy as an integral part of the royal family's Wahhabite-directed and tribal-supported rule. The upper class has been traditional in every aspect of its behavior: in the exercise of power, authority, and influence; in its adherence to tribal customs; and in its confession, interpretation, and defense of the Muslim faith. Moreover, it has perceived itself as the ordained guardian of the divine order of things in Arabia. Mysticism, a hierarchical structure, faith, and economic power have combined to keep this class in control for many decades. Whatever conflict or tension has existed within the upper class over the years has always been over personalities, never over the raison d'être or philosophy of the class itself.

The lower class in Saudi Arabia has normally included the majority of the nomadic bedouins, the unskilled workers and the land tenants in rural areas. This class has held no political power whatsoever; nor has it actively worked toward any societal change. The group has not perceived itself as a part of a nation; rather it has considered itself a part of much smaller tribal or familial units that are economically, politically, and socially self-sufficient.[17] In the middle of the spectrum, a very small middle class has traditionally

---

[16] Like other ruling classes in the Middle East, the Saudi upper class consists of a king, a ruling family, tribal nobility, landlords, the *'ulama*, and the military elite. For a useful discussion of this topic, see Bill, "Class Analysis and Dialectics," p. 428.

[17] Rugh, "Emergence of a New Middle Class in Saudi Arabia," p. 7.

existed in the country. It has consisted of a sprinkling of small shopkeepers, low-level civil servants, clerics, and artisans. It has wielded no power or influence; nor has it performed any functions which might have linked it to the influential stratum of the population.

Oil revenues and the expanding educational base have combined to create a new and diverse stratum of professionals, managers, administrators, adequately trained teachers, lawyers, army officers, pilots, skilled workers, electronics engineers and technicians, planners, corporate managers, and systems analysts. Due to the lack of adequate statistics, it is difficult to provide any quantification of this group, coming to be known as the new middle class, but it is possible to discern its existence as a separate class. The common characteristic of this class is its occupational foundation. It perceives itself and is perceived by others in terms of the functions it performs and the unquestioned need for these functions in the building of a modern state.

The importance of this class and the corresponding power position in which it finds itself are rooted in the necessity of and the demand for the occupations of members of this class. The specialized training which members of this class have acquired to qualify for these occupations bestows upon them special privileges; influence flows naturally from this privileged position and is based solely on the functions performed—an unprecedented phenomenon in a traditional society. Familial and other contacts, traditional prerequisites for acquiring an influential position, are less important conditions with the new middle class. Training, expertise and competence, not family background or tribal extraction, are the source of the new influence. This can be a shattering experience in a traditional society thrown, almost unwittingly, into the massive complexities of modernization. This linkage between power and employment underlies the "central conflict that marks the Middle East today." [18]

The new middle class exercises its authority through the ministerial positions and other high bureaucratic offices its members hold. Since no political parties exist in Saudi Arabia and since politics still remains the prerogative of the royal family through the person of the king, the new middle class exercises its influence more in economic policy making than in the political sphere.[19] Constitutional questions, indeed all major political questions, are the affair of the royal family. Even when a major economic policy is contemplated, the views of

---

[18] Bill, "Class Analysis and Dialectics," pp. 425 and 434.
[19] Rugh, "Emergence of a New Middle Class in Saudi Arabia," p. 20.

expert technocrats are solicited and considered, but the final decision rests with the king. As a corollary, the influence of any one technocrat on public policy at the national level is largely a function of the personal relationship between the technocrat and the king. This is obviously the case when the person in question is either a minister or a deputy minister.

Another marked characteristic of the new middle class in Saudi Arabia is that it includes an increasing number of younger, foreign-educated (mostly Western) and well-traveled royal princes. These princes are the sons and nephews of the Saud brothers and uncles who have ruled Saudi Arabia for over a generation, and technically they belong to the royal family or the upper class. Yet their secular orientation, attitudes on modernization, perceptions of nation building in the country, national consciousness, advanced education, and technical training have made them more attuned to the hopes and aspirations of the new middle class. These princes find themselves in the unique position of being able to exercise influence through three channels simultaneously: the royal family, the formal bureaucracy, and the new middle class.[20] As a special group and a unique elite within the new generation of Saudis, this group of princes will have a strong impact on the future course of Saudi politics.

The absence of organized political activity in the country, the sparsely distributed population and the nature of the country's terrain make it almost impossible, at least in the foreseeable future, for any major political upheaval or revolution to occur in Saudi Arabia.[21] Any political changes or socio-political reforms will be effected by the royal family and not necessarily as a result of popular demands. It is in the planning and execution of social and political reforms that the new group of princes, and through them the new middle class, will play a crucial role. The second five-year economic development plan and its resultant massive social and economic changes will provide the new princes with ample opportunities to assert their role. Societal harmony in a modern Saudi Arabia will very much depend on the ability of the new princes to synthesize modern education and Arabia's traditionalism. Social dislocations which are haphazardly planned and executed without careful study would give birth to a stillborn society.

In sum, the new middle class, although numerically small, has succeeded in penetrating the higher echelons of the governmental structure (see Table 7). Positive contributions have been made by this

---

[20] Ibid., pp. 17 20.

[21] For a more detailed discussion of this and related points, see David Holden, *Farewell to Arabia* (New York: Walker and Co., 1966).

Table 7

EDUCATIONAL BACKGROUND OF TOP SAUDI OFFICIALS, 1972

	Minister	Deputy Ministers
Ministries		
Interior	High school [a]	1) High school [a] 2) Cairo B.A. 3) High school [a]
Defense	High school [a]	High school [a]
Finance	High school [a]	Cairo B.A.
Foreign Affairs	Traditional [a]	1) U.S. B.A. 2) Cairo B.A.
Education	Traditional	1) U.S. B.A. [a] 2) U.S. Ph.D.
Commerce	Cairo B.A.	U.S. M.A.
Petroleum	U.S. M.A.	1) U.S. B.A. [a] 2) U.S. Ph.D.
Agriculture	U.S. M.A.	1) U.S. M.A. 2) U.S. B.A. [a] 3) Cairo B.A.
Health	Cairo B.A.	Cairo D.D.S.
Labor	Cairo B.A.	1) U.S. M.A. 2) U.S. Ph.D.
Information	Cairo B.A.	U.S. B.A. [a]
Communications	Traditional	1) Cairo B.A. 2) High school 3) U.S. M.A.
Pilgrimage	High school	Cairo B.A.
Justice	Traditional	Traditional
Major agencies [b]		
National Guard	Traditional [a]	Traditional [a]
Central Planning Org.	U.S. M.A.	U.S. Ph.D.
Petromin	U.S. Ph.D.	U.K. B.A. [a]
Gen. Personnel Bur.	U.S. M.A.	U.S. B.A.
Investigation Bur.	Cairo B.A.	Cairo M.A.
Major governorates		
Mecca	High school [a]	U.S. B.A. [a]
Riyadh	High school [a]	U.S. B.A. [a]
Medina	High school [a]	
Eastern Province	High school [a]	

[a] Members of the royal family.

[b] Headed by directors who hold minister of state rank and sit on the Council of Ministers.

Source: William Rugh, "Emergence of a New Middle Class in Saudi Arabia," *Middle East Journal*, Winter 1973, p. 16.

class to the process of modernization in the country, and there is no reason why this contribution should not continue. A synthesis of traditionalism and modernity can be successfully effected in Saudi Arabia despite the crisis of abundance. In order for this synthesis to function smoothly, the new middle class, especially the younger princes, must be brought into the decision-making process. The young princes are, by fact of training and education, qualified to assume more responsibility in the running of the state, and it is through them that the Saudi system of government will be able to outlive the brothers and uncles who founded the kingdom.

Goals and Options: Saudi Arabia

Concerning political development and the future of the monarchical institution in the country, Saudi Arabia's long-range plans center around the following five goals:

(1) Maintain a monarchical system of government controlled by the house of Saud in which the king performs three major roles simultaneously: the head of state, the chief imam, and the chief tribal sheikh.

(2) Allow for and even encourage a cautious and extremely gradual process of opening the regime to limited popular participation, initially through the route of a *majlis shura*, or consultative council.

(3) Adhere to the Koran and the *shari'a* as the basis of any state law or constitution.

(4) Reject all "foreign" ideologies (for example, communism, socialism, Zionism) as incompatible with Islam and as inapplicable to Saudi Arabia's domestic political development and stability.

(5) Maintain a hierarchical system of authority, with the king as the ultimate decision maker.

As has been indicated above, for the last two decades the statements and actions of the Saudi kings pertaining to internal political development have revolved around the preceding five goals. Political evolution in recent years has been inspired, decreed, and executed by the royal family, situated at the apex of the pyramid of power. Political reform has never been seriously or widely demanded from below. Demands for political reform in the late 1950s and early 1960s came from a group of Saudi princes who left Saudi Arabia for Egypt—later to return to the royal fold. These princes, who were led by Talal ibn 'Abd al-'Aziz, the king's younger brother, had called for a constitution and a limited form of an elected parliament. Their demands were rejected outright by Prime Minister Faysal.[22]

The primary objectives of Saudi monarchs since independence in 1932 have been to consolidate the authority and power of the royal family and to consolidate the authority of the individual king within the family. King 'Abd al-'Aziz (1932–53) established the supremacy of the royal family over the country. Political struggles and rivalries within the family between 1958 and 1964, specifically between Saud and Faysal, served to strengthen the authority of the king himself. As was stated earlier, King Saud failed to retain his authority, and in 1964 he was replaced by his brother Faysal. In this era of consolidation, as Saudi royalists have frequently pointed out, no popular participation or public dissent could have been tolerated. Political parties and organizations were equally nonexistent. More fundamental, however, is the fact that the Saudi monarchy, aside from its own conservatism, has been supported by the country's conservative elements: tribal sheikhs, the *'ulama,* and the *shari'a* judges. These three groups would presumably decline in influence as a result of any democratization of the regime.

Four factors acted to reinforce this alliance between the forces of conservatism and the Saudi kings:

(1) The level of illiteracy was extremely high.

(2) Higher education was limited to a few princes.

(3) Saudi Arabia has been a closed society, and foreign ideas, trends, and developments have been kept out of the country.

(4) No national consciousness existed among the majority of the population, the bedouin nomads, to whom the tribe or the village, not the government in Riyadh, was the readily identifiable social, political and economic unit.

The symbiotic relationship between the house of Saud and the conservative elements maintained domestic stability, and contacts with the outside world were mainly through the pilgrims who came to Mecca from throughout the world.

Social conditions in Saudi Arabia have changed. The factors which contributed to traditional political stability and to the successful alliance between the royal family and the conservative elements have for the most part ceased to exist. Although functional literacy is still very low, enormous strides have been made in education, and higher education is no longer the prerogative of princes. Thousands

---

[22] For an overall view of the story of the five princes and their political demands, see *Area Handbook for Saudi Arabia*, pp. 152-55.

of Saudis are enrolled in colleges and universities, both in Saudi Arabia and abroad, especially in the United States and Europe. Also because of oil and the resulting revenues and economic development in the country, Saudi Arabia is no longer a closed society; "foreign" ideas of government, constitutionalism, and individual freedom can no longer be kept at arm's length. Finally, like all nation-states, a spirit of national consciousness has begun to coalesce in Saudi Arabia; the idea of popular sovereignty is slowly but perceptibly gaining acceptance. The developing new middle class will probably hasten the opening up of the regime, perhaps faster than the royal family would wish. A definite process of change is occurring, unstoppable and irreversible.

In the face of this inevitable political change, what options are available to the Saudi monarchy which would enable it to achieve its long-range goals? Whatever course of action the royal family and King Khalid decide to follow, if the monarchy is to be preserved the family must comprehend the processes of change, control them, and thereby influence their outcome. King Khalid's new national political program, including his announced intention to establish a *majlis shura*, is a recognition of the inevitability of change.[23]

The king has also stated that the new political system, including the *majlis*, will be inspired by the Koran.[24] The new policy, King Khalid emphasized, would be a continuation of the policies of the late King Faysal.[25] The authority and composition of the new consultative assembly, once established, would obviously determine its future role in the process of political change. Saudi Arabia's neighbors in the lower gulf, Bahrain, Qatar, and the United Arab Emirates, have all established varying forms of assemblies, with Bahrain's popularly elected National Assembly being the most advanced system.

As the result of a constitutional crisis between the government and the National Assembly in the spring of 1975, the amir of Bahrain dissolved the assembly on 26 August 1975 and ordered a new election law written. In the midst of this political transformation of neighboring regimes, Saudi Arabia cannot remain a totally autocratic fortress for long.

In sum, it might be very difficult to strike a functional balance between Saudi-Islamic-Wahhabite tradition and the country's rapidly changing socioeconomic environment, but if the royal family is to

[23] *New York Times*, 1 April 1975.
[24] *Sada al-'Usbu'* (Bahrain), 8 April 1975, p. 16.
[25] *Washington Post*, 1 April 1975.

endure, if domestic stability is to be maintained, if participatory government is indeed the wave of the future, the royal family must search for the right balance between all of these new forces. Otherwise traditionalism will be swept away by the forces of change, and neither the Koran nor the *shari'a* will be able to withstand the onslaught.

Goals and Options: The United States

On the surface, political development within Saudi Arabia would seem irrelevant to American policy makers. A deeper analysis of this question, however, indicates precisely the opposite. Consider the following exchange which took place at a congressional hearing on the stability of oil supplies between Congressman Jonathan B. Bingham, member of the House Subcommittee on the Near East and South Asia, and Mr. John G. McLean, chairman and executive officer of the Continental Oil Company:

> Mr. Bingham: Do you have from your sources, or other company sources, an estimate of the stability, the political stability, of Saudi Arabia? If they were to go the route of Libya, we would really be in trouble, wouldn't we?
>
> Mr. McLean: Saudi Arabia sends 7 to 10 thousand young people a year, government financed, to study in Western Europe and the United States—at the University of California, Harvard, and Columbia. They go back with some different ideas on how the country ought to be run. In 10 years time, they will have moved into positions of power. So 10 years from now I think you will see a transformation in the Saudi Government for better or worse. You can't bank on what we have got today, I don't think.[26]

The above exchange is an excellent illustration of the United States's stake in the political future of Saudi Arabia. Whatever changes occur within the Saudi political system, they will obviously have an impact on the entire region. Therefore, because of an American interest in regional security and a continued flow of oil and because of the organic connection between Saudi domestic politics and its foreign policy, especially on regional security and oil matters, the United States observes Saudi politics very closely indeed. Evolutionary political reform under the auspices of the Saudi monarchy is,

---

[26] U.S. Congress, House of Representatives, Committee on Foreign Affairs, *Oil Negotiations, OPEC, and the Stability of Supply,* 93d Congress, 1st session (Washington, D. C.: U.S. Government Printing Office, 1973), p. 101.

according to American policy makers, the only sure formula for continued political stability in the kingdom. The United States and Saudi Arabia also have a common interest in their opposition to radicalism in the gulf region. The United States-Saudi Arabia Joint Commission on Security Cooperation testifies to the accord these countries have reached in maintaining regional political stability devoid of "foreign" ideologies—communism in particular.

In an off-the-record press interview which the late King Faysal gave in summer 1972 and which was published only after the king's assassination, the king emphasized the following points: (1) Foreign ideologies do not serve the interests of the Arab nation and Islam. (2) Communism is Islam's worst enemy. (3) Political radicalism in the gulf is supported by foreign ideologies.[27]

King Faysal was obviously referring to the Dhufari rebellion and other movements in the region. Based on this ideological view, Saudi Arabia has suppressed political dissent at home, has aided the Sultan of Oman against the Dhufari rebels, has acquiesced to Iran's military operations on behalf of the Sultan of Oman, has tolerated the United States naval presence in Bahrain, and has more recently looked with favor upon the United States Air Force presence on the Omani island of Masirah. The United States has thus far shared King Faysal's views, and stability and the containment of radicalism constitute the short-range and long-range goals of the United States toward political development in Saudi Arabia.

In terms of policy options, however, the United States must realize that the influx of thousands of Saudi college graduates, as McLean stated above, will in the next decade have a serious impact on the body politic of Saudi Arabia. The tidal wave of technically trained foreign nationals necessary for the second five-year economic development plan will also have significant effects on Saudi politics. If the primary function of knowledge and theory is to minimize surprise, then American and Saudi policy makers must jointly choose the option of assessing the direction and intensity of change, as embodied in the rising educated middle class, and of directing it on to the path of gradual political reform.

---

[27] *Sada al-'Usbu'* (Bahrain), 1 April 1975. At the request of King Faysal, the weekly withheld publication of this interview for almost three years.

3

THE STRATEGIC DIMENSION

An Overview

The United States's economic and political interests in Saudi Arabia
and the Arabian peninsula which were reviewed in the preceding two
chapters are an integral part of the United States strategic posture
toward the entire Arab/Persian Gulf region and the Red Sea basin.
Saudi Arabia will also continue to be a prime factor in America's
relations with Southwest Asia. The Saudi connection is an important
ingredient in American policy planning for several areas and issues:
the Red Sea and the Suez Canal, the Persian Gulf and the flow of oil,
the Indian Ocean and Soviet naval strategy east of Suez, the Arab-
Israeli conflict and the alternatives of war and peace, and the actual
United States military presence in the region. A new issue of rapidly
increasing importance for the United States in which Saudi Arabia
will also figure prominently is the unlooked-for rapprochement
between Iran and Iraq and the possibility of a radical reshaping of
the traditional assumptions of gulf security which have held firm for
over twenty years.

Due to its oil, wealth, size, geographic location, and newly found
economic power, Saudi Arabia is definitely involved in these areas
and issues of American foreign policy. Any rational analysis of
United States long-range policy goals and options toward the region
must therefore necessarily take the Saudi presence into consideration.
Until this is done with some awareness of the new political, economic,
military, and diplomatic realities of the region, American long-range
policy planning will just muddle through with no clear end in sight.

Planning an American long-range foreign policy toward Saudi
Arabia, the Middle East, and the Persian Gulf must take into account

several new realities. First, Saudi Arabia is on its way to becoming a financial giant with an annual income in excess of $25 billion; over 50 percent of these revenues cannot be absorbed into the country's economy. Second, in addition to being a major holder of billions of unspent dollars, and probably because of it, Saudi Arabia is fast becoming a major importer of American arms, military equipment, technology, and personnel. Lest we lose sight of the larger implications of this question, Iran, just across the gulf from Saudi Arabia, is perhaps the best customer of the American defense industry.

Third, in its quest for rapid, massive economic development, Saudi Arabia will need to accommodate tens of thousands of foreign technical and managerial experts; the United States is regarded as a major source of this needed manpower. Fourth, with the opening of the Suez Canal, the Red Sea basin, after almost a decade of inactivity, is rapidly assuming fresh strategic significance. With the presence of the People's Democratic Republic of Yemen (PDRY) at the Bab al-Mandab entrance to the Red Sea and with the Eritrean insurgency and the unpredictable policies of the post-imperial regime in Ethiopia, Saudi Arabia could once again act as a stabilizing factor in this region.[1] Fifth, American strategists would like to expand the U.S. military presence in the form of new facilities in the Indian Ocean and around the Strait of Hormuz, the entrance to the Persian Gulf. This presence is made visible in the expanded communications facilities on Diego Garcia island in the Indian Ocean,[2] in the recently concluded landing agreement for Masirah Island, and in expanding military arrangements with the Sultan of Oman.

The American naval facility in Bahrain and future agreements between the United States and Bahrain on this matter are another aspect of the American military presence. Again, Saudi Arabia's present and future positions on the question of the American military presence in the immediate region is and will be very important.

The most fundamental new reality by far is the 6 March 1975 Iranian-Iraqi agreement to settle their generations-old boundary dispute. Iraq was able to overcome two serious disabilities by this agreement. It put an end to the Kurdish war in the north, and it

---

[1] For a discussion of the strategic significance of the Red Sea basin, see John Duke Anthony, *The Red Sea: Control of the Southern Approach*, Middle East Problem Paper No. 13 (Washington, D. C.: The Middle East Institute, January 1975).

[2] U.S. Congress, House of Representatives, Committee on Foreign Affairs, *Proposed Expansion of U.S. Military Facilities in the Indian Ocean*, 93d Congress, 2d session (Washington, D. C.: U.S. Government Printing Office, 1974).

emerged from its relative political isolation in the gulf. The sudden momentum of Iraq's newly pragmatic, gulf-oriented diplomacy has created a whirlwind of diplomatic activity and a flurry of new bilateral reconciliation agreements over many disputed boundaries. Any possible collective-security pacts in the region might include Iraq, Iran, and Saudi Arabia, an unthinkable entente only a few months ago. The United States, as the major supplier of arms to both Saudi Arabia and Iran and as a major importer of oil from both, will certainly observe these developing diplomatic linkages with more than casual interest.

There is another set of factors which enter into American-Saudi strategic considerations and which involve American interests in the region. Traditionally these interests have centered around four main points: (1) Support of indigenous regional cooperative efforts and the collective security and orderly economic progress of the area, (2) encouragement of peaceful resolution of territorial and other disputes among states and widening channels of communication and consultation between them, (3) expanding U.S. diplomatic, cultural, technical, commercial and financial presence and activities, and (4) maintaining access to the area's oil supplies at reasonable prices.[3]

Implicit in these statements has always been one primary objective: keeping the region free of extensive Soviet influence. The United States has usually equated this feared Soviet threat with such radical political movements as the Popular Front for the Liberation of Oman and the Iraqi Ba'thist regime. Accordingly, the United States has assisted local governments in fighting radicalism and has actively engaged in a diplomatic campaign to isolate Ba'thist Iraq from the gulf by promoting closer triangular ties between the United States, Saudi Arabia, and Iran.

Ideological Supports of Saudi Arabia's Foreign Policy

Saudi Arabia's foreign policy has been predicated upon three simple but forceful ideologies: a strong defense of Islam, Koranic traditions and teachings and Islamic holy places, a staunch opposition to communism, internationally and regionally, and unwavering support of the Palestinian people in their quest for a national identity in Palestine. In its active defense of Islam, Saudi Arabia has championed the cause of Muslims all over the world in such diverse places as

---

[3] Department of State, Bureau of Public Affairs, *U.S. Relations with Arabian Peninsula/Persian Gulf Countries* (Washington, D. C.: U.S. Government Printing Office, 1974), p. 2.

Indonesia, the Philippines, Pakistan, central Africa and the Soviet Union. It has also strongly condemned Israel's occupation of East Jerusalem; a recurring wish of the late King Faysal was to be able to pray in the Mosque of Omar in Jerusalem, the third holiest shrine of Islam.

A professed objective of the 1973–74 oil embargo was to generate American pressure on Israel to relinquish the occupied territories, especially Jerusalem. In April 1975, Sheikh Yamani stated that the oil weapon was set aside only temporarily; it might be used later if the Arab-Israeli impasse is not resolved.[4] Saudi Arabia, according to Yamani, was interested in the peaceful solution of the conflict.

The Saudi government's opposition to communism has contributed to a foreign policy based on close cooperation with the United States and other Western powers and on a refusal to open any serious dialogue with the Soviet Union, mainland China, or other Communist countries. Saudi Arabia has always believed that communism and related ideologies are inimical to Islam, a theme that ran through King Faysal's official speeches and pronouncements.[5] Closer to home, Saudi Arabia's kings, especially King Faysal, have strongly condemned leftist and/or "alien" ideologies in the gulf and the Arab world. King Faysal actively opposed the leftist-socialist regime in South Yemen, the Dhufari rebellion against the Sultan of Oman, and the activities of the Popular Front for the Liberation of Oman throughout the gulf. Moreover, relations with the Ba'thist regime in Iraq have been extremely cool. Conversely, the Saudi government has supported the conservative tribal regimes of the peripheral states of Arabia.

On Palestine the Saudi government has taken a forceful stand, especially since the October War of 1973. Prior to 1973, Saudi Arabia had resisted all urgings to use oil for political ends. Separation of oil and politics was the operative principle of Saudi foreign policy. The situation radically changed in October 1973, and it culminated in the oil embargo. In addition to this economic action, Saudi Arabia has generously financed the military operations of those states in "confrontation" with Israel, primarily Egypt and Syria, and has also financed some of the arms purchases for them. Riyadh has also given

---

[4] *Washington Post*, 23 April 1975.

[5] Kingdom of Saudi Arabia, Ministry of Information, *Faysal Speaks: Book XII* (Jidda: no publisher, no date). See also King Faysal's address to the pilgrims in Mecca, 20 December 1974, thought to be the king's last public address; Kingdom of Saudi Arabia, Ministry of Information, *Royal Speech: December 20, 1974* (Jidda: Dar al-Asfahani and Company, no date).

direct financial support to the Palestine Liberation Organization. These policies have been continued by King Khalid.[6]

The ideological supports of Saudi foreign policy closely correspond to the three concentric circles in which Saudi foreign policy has been most active: the gulf-Arab circle, the Islamic circle and the Western-international circle. It is obvious that oil-generated wealth constitutes the power factor that has enabled Saudi Arabia since 1973 to engage in an active foreign policy in support of its ideological principles and within its spheres of activity.

Arms and Power

As a reflection of its relations with the United States and of its desire to translate oil wealth into power, Saudi Arabia has launched two large-scale operations: internal economic development and the building of a modern army. The United States has been called upon to assist in both areas. The United States-Saudi Arabia joint economic and security commissions are the agents of choice to implement cooperation in both areas. The commissions also indicate Saudi Arabia's increasing stature in world affairs and, more importantly, the identity of American-Saudi interests in these areas. Since economic cooperation was discussed earlier, attention will be given to the arms buildup in Saudi Arabia and to the questions which this buildup has generated.

Whether it is termed an arms race, arms trade or defense contracting, one thing has become obvious: the Persian Gulf countries, notably Iran and Saudi Arabia, are arming themselves to the teeth, on a cash-and-carry basis, with American arms and weapons systems.[7] Most of this arms buildup in Iran and Saudi Arabia started only a few years ago, but the current level was not reached until 1973–74, coincident with the advent of substantial oil revenues.[8]

---

[6] *al-Adwa'* (Bahrain), 10 April 1975.

[7] For a selection of press reports on this point consider the following headlines: "The Persian Gulf Has a Deadly Little Arms Race," *New York Times*, 15 December 1974; "Arms for Sale: The Persian Gulf," *Washington Post*, 10 November 1974; "Selling Arms in the Persian Gulf," *Washington Post*, 25 January 1975; "Imperial Iran," *Washington Post*, 30 December 1974; and Jack Anderson, "Whatever the Shah Wants, the Shah Gets," *Washington Post*, 19 January 1975. For a very informative comparative study of arms in the region, see Dale R. Tahtinen, *Arms in the Persian Gulf* (Washington, D. C.: American Enterprise Institute, 1974).

[8] For a comprehensive picture of the arms buildup in Iran, see *The Military Balance, 1974-1975* (London: The International Institute for Strategic Studies, 1974), pp. 31-40.

According to *The Military Balance, 1974–1975*, Saudi Arabia's regular armed forces and national guard in 1974 totaled 69,000 (army: 36,000; navy: 1,500; air force: 5,500; national guard: 26,000). The 1974–75 defense expenditures totaled over $1.8 billion.[9] This represented more than a 22 percent increase over the 1973 military budget.[10] During 1973–74, Saudi Arabia had on order in Britain, France, and the United States military equipment which included tanks, fighters, frigates, minesweepers, and HAWK (SAM) missiles.[11] These orders, which could be conservatively estimated at over $1 billion, did not include the complex web of bilateral service agreements concluded between Saudi Arabia and the United States since June 1974.

In testimony before the House Subcommittee on the Near East and South Asia in August 1974, Richard R. Violette, director for sales negotiations at the Defense Security Assistance Agency, stated that American military programs in Saudi Arabia covered "a fairly broad range."[12] The United States has agreed to provide services for Saudi Arabia in the following areas: sale of F-5 fighter jets, buildup of the navy, modernization of the national guard, construction of an air-defense capability, and engineering and construction management services.[13] Still more agreements are contemplated under the United States–Saudi Arabia Joint Commission on Security Cooperation, including the exchange of announced and unannounced visits by high officials of both countries for purposes of ongoing coordination and consultation.

Serious questions are now being raised in regard to the massive sale of sophisticated weapons systems to Iran and Saudi Arabia. These questions concern the long-range implications of these agreements, the ultimate uses of the weapons, the doubtful ability of Iran and Saudi Arabia to effectively employ the weapons, and the ever-present possibility of arms transfers to other countries. Other questions have dealt with the ultimate moral and ethical questions embedded in this entire issue. Some have called for reassessment of all arms sales,[14] especially the massive sales to Iran; others have advocated arms

[9] Ibid., p. 37.

[10] Ibid., p. 79.

[11] Ibid., p. 90.

[12] U.S. Congress, House, Committee on Foreign Affairs, *The Persian Gulf, 1974*, p. 7.

[13] Ibid. See pages 7-9 for U.S. military programs in Iran and other gulf countries.

[14] Tahtinen, *Arms in the Persian Gulf*, pp. 30-31.

control;[15] still others have demanded congressional scrutiny of all substantial arms agreements.[16]

Several rationales have been presented by defenders of arms sales. The arms will protect the recipients against possible threats. The sales will tighten relations between the United States and the purchasers. If Saudi Arabia (or neighboring states for that matter) did not buy American arms, it would shop somewhere else and a worsening of the United States balance of payments would result. Also the sale of arms and the involvement of American personnel in training programs would expand and deepen American influence in those countries. It should be noted that most of these arms-sale agreements are regarded by the executive branch as executive agreements, negotiated without the advice and consent of Congress.

The persistent uncertainty over the ultimate use of these weapons arsenals in the Persian Gulf and the lack of effective guidelines covering the sale of these arms have contributed to the prevailing mood of frustration in Congress and are cogent reasons why the entire question of large-scale arms sales should be examined fully. Such an examination must resolve at least five sets of questions:

(1) What is the nature of the threat which is supposedly hovering over countries like Saudi Arabia and Iran such that the United States finds itself obliged to sell them arms? Is it an external threat or is it an internal threat supported by elements interested in destroying or reforming the present regimes?

(2) Is the sale of arms the only economically viable and enticing method for improving the United States balance of trade, or can petrodollars be more peacefully retrieved through such investment channels as treasury securities, corporate investments, and expansion of exports and the sale of industrial equipment?

(3) Will these arms be stockpiled in Saudi Arabia, or will they be transferred to third party countries? Also since the Saudi armed forces will require several years before they are able to absorb the military technology to employ these weapons systems, will they be manned by American military technical advisors or will they be allowed to deteriorate before they are ever used?

---

[15] Robert J. Pranger, *Towards Arms Control in the Middle East*, Middle East Problem Paper No. 9 (Washington, D. C.: The Middle East Institute, October 1974).

[16] In a letter to President Ford on 20 December 1974 concerning the United States arms sale to Iran, Congressman Clarence D. Long (D-Maryland) strongly criticized the sale of arms to Iran on three grounds: the depletion of American technical skills, the depletion of American hardware, and the secrecy of American commitments to Iran. Copies of the letter were released by the congressman's office on 2 January 1975.

(4) Might the advent of these arms and the intensive training programs for Saudi army officers create an elitist, politically sensitive and potentially influential class of army officers? Have American policy makers studied the long-range impact of this new class on Saudi society? Will the officer class contribute to an evolutionary process of political change or will it be a destabilizing factor in society?

(5) Will the newly acquired weapons really function as an effective deterrent to potential external aggression or threats of aggression? Is there a possibility that Saudi Arabia might one day find itself in a military conflict with Iran, which is also armed and trained by American advisors?

Answers to these questions are long overdue. These are worrisome questions and real issues which will not vanish overnight; the rationale that if we do not sell them arms somebody else will no longer suffices. The accumulation of sophisticated weaponry in such a highly volatile region can almost surely lead to only one end, an explosive conflict over which the United States might have little control and which would jeopardize American interests.

Oil Brinkmanship

Two new diplomatic developments have recently engaged the attention of the oil producers and will undoubtedly leave long-lasting impressions on producers and consumers alike. The first can be best described as Secretary Kissinger's brinkmanship on the possible use of force to insure an uninterrupted flow of oil. The second is the unexpected Iraqi-Iranian rapprochement.

In an age of international economic interdependence, the threat of force to resolve a dispute over oil would have been dismissed outright as one of Secretary Kissinger's musings, except that this hypothetical possibility was also raised by President Ford and by Secretary of Defense Schlesinger. Since some orchestration seemed to have been arranged between official pronouncements and similar statements by certain academicians on the subject, and since Saudi Arabia viewed these pronouncements as a serious threat, one can no longer disregard this viewpoint.

Simply stated, Secretary Kissinger's hypothesis on the possible use of force in the face of economic strangulation, which was expressed in an interview published in *Business Week* in January 1975,[17]

---

[17] *Business Week*, 13 January 1975.

was based on four assumptions: (1) Another Arab oil embargo similar to the one imposed in 1973 would essentially strangulate the industrial world, including the United States, (2) the right of nation-states to defend themselves against the threat of strangulation, (3) the likely need to use force against the embargo-supporting states in order to obtain oil, and (4) the desirability of openly discussing such a possibility.

A few days following the *Business Week* interview, Secretary Kissinger said: "I was speaking hypothetically about an extreme situation. . . . We were not talking, as is so loosely said, about the seizure of oil fields. That is not our intention. That is not our policy."[18] Despite this disclaimer and the negative reaction of the American people,[19] two other major articles appeared within two months' time advocating the option of military action against the oil producers in the event of an oil embargo.

The article which stirred noticeable controversy was written by Robert W. Tucker.[20] The other article was written by a "Washington-based professor and a defense consultant" under the pseudonym of Miles Ignotius.[21] Both writers concluded that it was indeed feasible to mount a military operation against certain oil fields on the Arab littoral of the Persian Gulf. Like Kissinger, both writers concluded with "deadly logic" that the United States could not withstand another oil embargo. The same theme was reiterated by Secretary of Defense Schlesinger in May 1975.[22]

The defense of possible American military action against the oil producers is based on three points. First, since it would be difficult to curb America's energy demands, the United States should contemplate the use of force to secure the source of energy, primarily Persian Gulf oil fields. Second, it would be militarily feasible to launch a brief, effective military operation to occupy the 400-mile-long strip of oil fields between Kuwait and Qatar with minimum cost. Finally, even if the oil producers should blow up the wells during the operation, it can be argued that under American occupation the wells could be repaired in three to twelve months.

---

[18] An interview given by Kissinger on "Bill Moyers' Journal: International Report," reproduced by the Department of State's Bureau of Public Affairs as *The Secretary-of-State Interview*, 16 January 1975, p. 6.

[19] Only 10 percent of those interviewed by the Gallup Poll supported military action. "Mideast Invasion by U.S. Opposed," *Washington Post*, 23 January 1975.

[20] "Oil: The Issue of American Intervention," *Commentary*, January 1975, reproduced in the *Washington Post*, 5 January 1975.

[21] "Seizing Arab Oil," *Harper's*, March 1975, pp. 45-62.

[22] *Washington Post*, 19 May 1975.

Although this course of action may be tempting to some as a simple, efficient solution to complex economic problems, it has several underlying weaknesses. Those who advocate military action assume that the oil-producing countries are a tightly knit group, located in the same region and sharing the same ideology. In reality, OPEC spans the globe from Venezuela to Indonesia and encompasses the whole range of political ideologies and regimes. It is certainly debatable whether military occupation of a 400-mile strip would emasculate OPEC or undermine its solidarity.

Possible military action in the Persian Gulf raises still another issue. Since the United States is in the ironic position of being the major source of arms and military advisors for Saudi Arabia and Iran, the gulf's two most prestigious policemen, an American invasion force would seem to be self-defeating.

Legally, the use of force to settle oil disputes would undermine the United Nations Charter. Article 33 directs the parties to any dispute to "seek a solution by negotiation, enquiry, mediation, conciliation, arbitration, judicial settlement, resort to regional agencies or arrangements, or other peaceful means of their own." The use of force in this dispute would greatly damage America's moral leadership in the world.

Politically, the militarists' argument is again on shaky ground. The new countries of the Persian Gulf have been engaged in building political communities based on some form of popular participation. Kuwait, Bahrain, Qatar, and the United Arab Emirates have all promulgated constitutions, and slowly but surely popular input is being felt in government. Kuwait and Bahrain have already held parliamentary elections and have functioning national assemblies. These political communities espouse moderation and evolutionary change. They have shunned radicalism from any side. The United States has encouraged these new governments on the path of moderation, and they have nearly stemmed the tide of radicalism in their region. The use of force or the threat of force in this area, no matter how hypothetical the possibility might be, would surely undermine moderation and promote radicalism—something the United States has been trying to avert for a generation.

It might be militarily possible to conduct a clinical strike and take over some of the oil wells along the coasts of Kuwait, Saudi Arabia, Qatar, Bahrain, and the United Arab Emirates before those countries succeeded in totally destroying their wells. But what would this accomplish? First, it would not guarantee the United States any more oil than it now imports, at lower prices than it now pays or with faster delivery than it now receives. America would be branded as an aggressor, and rightly so, without having gained any assurances of a more secure flow of oil. Also, a military operation could not necessarily be limited to a shallow coastal strip. It would most certainly enflame the Arab-Israeli conflict, make the Soviet Union more nervous, stir up North Africa and pit every OPEC country against the United States. Moreover, if Iraq, Iran, Saudi Arabia, and Oman entered the conflict, the terrain would change radically. The rugged hills, mountains and deserts of these countries are far more difficult to secure than the narrow treeless coast which figures so prominently in the militarists' argument.

From an economic perspective, the argument for military action again lies on poor ground. Quite simply, if the oil-producing countries in the gulf find themselves facing imminent military attack, they would destroy their wells. They can do without the wells for a while; the United States cannot. Instead of saving the world economy by the use of force, the United States, depending on the time it takes to repair the damage and resume the flow of oil, could create economic chaos of global proportions.

In retrospect, Secretary Kissinger's brinkmanship did not produce any tangible results. The prices did not go down; OPEC did not disintegrate; the consuming nations did not form a real front. Co-operation remains the only wise course of action. Last year's Saudi proposal for a meeting of consumers and producers is a logical step on the road to further cooperation, and it is encouraging that the United States has finally come to support this step.[23] In commenting on Secretary Kissinger's strangulation hypothesis, Leslie H. Gelb's apt comment on the "rule of folly" is worth quoting. He wrote: "The unthinkable had been thought and said out loud. It has been found to be militarily feasible and highly risky—and remote, hypothetical and chimerical."[24]

A New Diplomacy

Setting aside Secretary Kissinger's approach to the brink, the Iraqi-Iranian rapprochement may well constitute the cornerstone of a new diplomacy in the gulf. The agreement that was reached by the Shah

[23] It was announced during the Shah of Iran's visit to Washington in May 1975 that a meeting of representative consumers and producers would be held to discuss the future of energy. An Associated Press report in the *Frederick Post*, 19 May 1975.

[24] Leslie H. Gelb, "Why Did Mr. Kissinger Say That?" *New York Times*, 19 January 1975.

of Iran and Saddam Husayn, vice president of Iraq's Revolutionary Command Council, during the OPEC summit in Algiers on 6 March 1975 dealt with settling the boundary between the two countries at Shatt al-'Arab. The successful efforts of Algeria's President Houari Boumediene to bring the sides together signaled the end of a nagging conflict which has occasionally pushed the two countries to the point of open warfare. The conflict over the joint boundary has resulted from the different interpretations given to the 1937 Treaty by Iraq and Iran.[25]

The diplomatic implications of the new agreement cannot be overstated. At least five implications may be discerned from this agreement. First, by putting an end to the Kurdish rebellion, Iraq has freed its resources and its energies for influence abroad; the psychological boost to the Iraqi leadership cannot be exaggerated. Second, the advent of Iraq into gulf politics has depolarized gulf diplomacy; Iran and Saudi Arabia are no longer the only powers of the gulf. Third, the Iraqi-Iranian rapprochement has presented a less radical image of Iraq's Ba'thist ideology to the traditional rulers of Kuwait, Saudi Arabia, and the lower gulf.[26] Fourth, this rapprochement has generated a new attitude of reconciliation among gulf leaders which has led to new boundary agreements (Iraq and Saudi Arabia, Saudi Arabia and Kuwait, Kuwait and Iraq). Fifth, the return of Iraq to the gulf fold and the improved image of the shah among gulf Arabs have given rise to new speculations concerning a possible regional security pact of gulf powers. This possibility has stimulated a flurry of official visits in recent months.[27]

The leaders of Iran and Iraq view their countries as protectors of security and peace in the gulf. "The security of the Gulf states is the responsibility of the Gulf states as a whole," said Iraq's Saddam Husayn.[28] He also stated that Iraq was interested in a regional security arrangement with Iran, and he felt that Iraqi-Iranian rela-

---

[25] For a synopsis of the legal status of Shatt al-'Arab under international law, see Majid Khadduri, ed., *Major Middle Eastern Problems in International Law* (Washington, D. C.: American Enterprise Institute, 1972), pp. 88-94.

[26] For a representative analysis of the favorable reaction which the Iranian-Iraqi agreement has received see *al-Adwa'*, 8 May 1975.

[27] Bahrain's prime minister visits Iran (*Sada al-'Usbu'*, 13 May 1975); Bahrain's heir apparent visits Iraq (*al-Adwa'*, 1 May 1975); Kuwait's prime minister visits Bahrain, Qatar and the United Arab Emirates (*Sada al-'Usbu'*, 13 May 1975); Kuwait's prime minister visits Saudi Arabia (*al-Bahrayn al-Yom*, 12 May 1975); Saddam Husayn visits U.A.E. (*al-Adwa'*, 8 May 1975); U.A.E. foreign minister, Ahmad Khalifa al-Suwaydi, visits Bahrain and Iran (*al-Bahryn al-Yom*, 7 May 1975); and Saddam Husayn visits Iran (*al-Adwa'*, 8 May 1975).

[28] "Iraq Tries to Boost Gulf Security," *Washington Post*, 25 April 1975.

tions were "proceeding in such a way as to reduce the search for procurement of arms." [29]

Similar views were expressed by the shah. "The peace of the Gulf must be maintained by the states that adjoin its shores." [30] In his defense of new gulf "security structures," the shah obviously does not have in mind any direct role for either the United States or the Soviet Union. Since the United States is the only one of the two superpowers to have established a physical presence, small as it may be, in the gulf, it would be safe to expect that new pressures would be put on Bahrain to reassess its agreement with the United States.

Ironically, in 1971 the Bahraini ruling family looked upon the American naval presence at Jufair as a psychological protection for its newly achieved independence against possible territorial claims by Iran. Today, in the spirit of nationalism and with Iran's blessing, Bahrain might see fit to terminate the naval-facility agreement with the United States. Whether this comes to pass or not, the United States must itself reassess the continued usefulness of the navy's agreement with Bahrain.

Goals and Options: Saudi Arabia

Saudi Arabia has definite goals regarding its regional posture. The first goal is to maintain regional economic and political stability through free shipping and friendly neighboring regimes. The Saudi government realizes that its economic power would be seriously hampered if international shipping were to be interrupted. The government also realizes, and has frequently so stated, that international economic stability, particularly in the industrial world, is generically related to Saudi domestic prosperity.

Politically, Saudi Arabia perceives a logical relationship between its own conservative political system and status-quo-supporting regimes in the region. Riyadh has equated political stability with Islam, and it has supported the former and staunchly defended the latter. Saudi Arabia has also worked toward the establishment of a Saudi political hegemony on the Arab littoral of the gulf and has supported closer economic and political cooperation among the region's Arab states.[31]

---

[29] Ibid.

[30] "Iran Assuming Britain's Former Role as Guardian of Persian Gulf States," *New York Times*, 7 May 1975.

[31] *al-Adwa'* (Bahrain), 27 March 1975.

Saudi Arabia's Arab-world goals have centered around its support of the Palestinian cause against Israel; it has literally financed the Palestinian revolution.[32] Riyadh also believes that injustice was done to the Palestinians and that peaceful resolution of the conflict is the only guarantee for lasting peace in the region. Like communism, Zionism has been viewed by Saudi kings as an anti-Islam, alien ideology.

Militarily, Saudi Arabia believes that in order to have the ability to defend Islam and to defend itself against potential aggression from regimes and/or ideologies, it must become a respectable military power. Prince 'Abdalla ibn 'Abd al-'Aziz, head of the national guard, stated in March 1975 that military force is a guarantor of peace. As a supporter of the classical concept of power politics, he also mentioned that military might may be used as an arm of diplomacy. He was referring to the Arab-Israeli conflict and the failure of Kissinger's efforts to bring about a second Israeli-Egyptian territorial agreement.[33]

In order to achieve its goals, Saudi Arabia has chosen several policy options. In the area of international economics, Riyadh has been active simultaneously on four fronts: it has conditionally supported oil price cuts; it has advocated a conference of oil producers and consumers;[34] it has invested relatively heavily in Western industrial countries; and it has extended developmental loans to less developed countries, both unilaterally and through international agencies.

As regards regional security, Saudi Arabia has tacitly supported Iran's policeman role and has itself developed a policeman's role on the Arab side of the gulf in support of political conservatism. Riyadh has also worked toward the resolution of territorial conflicts with its neighbors (with Abu Dhabi over Buraymi and with Iraq over the neutral zone). It has also militarily and financially supported the Sultan of Oman against the Dhufari rebels. Saudi Arabia has recently shown some active support for the Iranian-Iraqi rapproachement and will most likely participate in any tripartite security structure with Iraq and Iran.

Although Saudi Arabia, like Iran and Iraq, has put forth the thesis that gulf security is the concern of gulf states only, it has cooperated closely with the United States and acquiesced in the expanding American role in the region. In addition to the costly bilateral defense procurement arrangements with the United States, Saudi Arabia has accepted the broad American concept of regional

---

[32] *New York Times*, 1 April 1975.

[33] *al-Adwa'* (Bahrain), 27 March 1975.

[34] *Washington Post*, 14 October 1974.

security, in particular the United States's view of the gulf as an extension of the Indian Ocean. Also, Saudi Arabia has tacitly approved of the American naval presence in Bahrain, American military aid to Sultan Qabus and the United States use of Omani bases at Masirah Island, Ra's Musandam, and elsewhere.[35]

In terms of future options, Saudi Arabia will perhaps consider the following courses of action:

(1) Working toward closer cooperation with the oil consumers.

(2) Expansion of its economic and technical cooperation with the industrial countries of the West.

(3) Re-examination of its current policy on arms buildup and reflection on the political implications of a potentially well-trained and highly equipped army.

(4) A more active role in the search for a regional security structure with Iran and Iraq.

(5) Commitment to a more active role in the search for a peaceful resolution of outstanding Arab conflicts, primarily the Palestine conflict and the Dhufari rebellion.

Saudi Arabia has the resources and the potential to play a leading role in regional peace and security. With careful policy planning and cooperation with its neighbors, it can share in the creation of a mutually protective regional hegemony.

Goals and Options: The United States

Since World War II the United States has had constant strategic interests all around Saudi Arabia, in the Indian Ocean,[36] on the island of Bahrain, in Ethiopia, on the African littoral of the Red Sea, and more recently in Oman. In 1974–75 the United States participated in clearing the Suez Canal, thereby underlining the strategic importance of that waterway.[37] The United States has also carefully monitored Soviet naval movements in the Indian Ocean and in the Persian Gulf and has sent its MIDEASTFOR from Bahrain on flag-showing,

---

[35] See a special analysis of the expanding American presence in the Gulf in *Sada al-'Usbu'* (Bahrain), 4 March 1975.

[36] U.S. Congress, House, Committee on Foreign Affairs, *Proposed Expansion of U.S. Military Facilities in the Indian Ocean.*

[37] U.S. Congress, House of Representatives, Committee on Foreign Affairs, *The United States Role in Opening the Suez Canal,* 93d Congress, 2d session (Washington, D. C.: U.S. Government Printing Office, 1974).

friendly visits to ports in states adjoining the Indian Ocean, from Ethiopia to Pakistan.[38]

For the most part, Saudi Arabia played an inconsequential role in American strategic policies during this period, and Saudi oil was not too greatly needed by the United States during the 1950s and 1960s. During the 1950s even Saudi Arabia itself had little control over its oil, especially after it had left Saudi ports. Aramco was the primary decision maker. Even after the founding of OPEC in 1960, the oil producers, including Saudi Arabia, continued to exercise very little control over oil policy. The producers began to exercise their OPEC power in 1971, when the first major pricing and participation agreements were signed.

The beginning of Saudi Arabia's crucial role in American strategy in terms of the Middle East and the Persian Gulf may be traced to the fall of 1972, when the phrase "energy crisis" first invaded the public consciousness. But it was not until after the October War and the oil embargo of 1973–74 that American strategists began to pay serious attention to Saudi Arabia. To date, there are six new considerations which have come to influence American strategic thinking and planning in the 1970s regarding Saudi Arabia and the Persian Gulf:

(1) This is an era of detente and expanding national consciousness among all nations, even in the Communist world. The monolithic view of communism which prevailed during the 1950s is no longer valid.

(2) Rapidly dwindling American domestic energy resources mean a corresponding increase in oil imports.

(3) The oil-producing states are emerging as states of significant wealth and economic power.

(4) Gulf societies, including Saudi Arabia, have undergone dramatic changes in the last decade—politically, demographically, and economically.

(5) The United States is indulging in massive arms sales to the gulf states, primarily Saudi Arabia and Iran, and there is a rapidly expanding American role in the training and modernization of the armed forces of these societies.

(6) Since the October War there has been a basic shift in the

---

[38] U.S. Congress, House of Representatives, Committee on Foreign Affairs, *Means of Measuring Naval Power with Special Reference to U.S. and Soviet Activities in the Indian Ocean* (Washington, D. C.: U.S. Government Printing Office, 1974), prepared for the Subcommittee on the Near East and South Asia of the Committee on Foreign Affairs by the Foreign Affairs Division, Congressional Research Service, Library of Congress.

Arab psychology toward Israel and an equally basic shift in American-Israeli relations.

In light of these developments, American long-range goals regarding Saudi Arabia may be summarized as follows:

(1) An uninterrupted flow of Saudi oil to the United States.

(2) Return of a significant portion of Saudi petrodollars to the United States in the form of pay for services rendered, arms, general trade, investment in U.S. Treasury bonds, and other forms of investment.

(3) Continued Saudi support of the United States role in the search for a peaceful resolution of the Palestine conflict.

(4) Continuation of the Saudi "moderating" influence among the states of the gulf region.

(5) Continued Saudi support of the United States position that the gulf should remain free from Soviet, Chinese, or other Communist influence.

In order to realize these five goals, the United States has selected the following policies:

(1) The United States has agreed to the Saudi proposal to convene a conference of oil producers and oil consumers. Washington is also currently discussing with Riyadh the possibility of signing a long-term oil agreement under which the United States would be guaranteed specified quantities of oil at a specified price. Moreover, the United States has attempted to convince the Saudis not to cut their oil production drastically to keep the price up.

(2) Washington has signed numerous bilateral agreements with Riyadh under which the United States would provide Saudi Arabia with services, technology, and equipment. The United States-Saudi Arabia Joint Commissions on Economic and Security Cooperation are but one aspect of United States efforts to retrieve some of its oil money. The United States has also strongly encouraged the Saudi government to purchase U.S. Treasury bonds.

(3) The United States has become Saudi Arabia's major source of arms and has supported the Saudi political ideology in the region.

(4) The United States has also become Iran's major source of arms, supporting Iranian influence in the gulf with the tacit approval of Saudi Arabia.

(5) In order to maintain its presence in the region, the United States has used Saudi influence to maintain its naval facility in Bahrain and to obtain an agreement from the Sultan of Oman for an aircraft landing site on Masirah Island.

4

TOWARD A STABLE PARTNERSHIP

For any American-Saudi relationship to function effectively and in a predictable fashion it must be based on mutual understanding of the long-range interests of each partner. Since the nation-state remains the primary unit of action in international relations, it is expected that both Saudi Arabia and the United States will constantly attempt to maximize their national interest. Therefore the policy options which each of the two states selects during a specific period and under specific circumstances would be expected to serve the long-range goals of each state's national interest. The discussion throughout this study has attempted to show that Saudi Arabia and the United States have several basic interests in common and are in the process of developing a functional framework for the realization of them. Policy makers in both countries have come to realize that the two countries' mutual interests can best be served through a system of partnership clearly and openly defined.[1]

Since oil is the underpinning of American-Saudi relations, all agreements and understandings between the two countries revolve, in one way or another, around this indispensable natural resource. Economic, commercial, educational, technological, financial and strategic agreements with Saudi Arabia are all a function of oil, of Riyadh's new wealth, and of American dependence on both of them. For the growing web of agreements between the two countries to be controlled and implemented successfully, at least five prerequisites must be present:

(1) A true American understanding of Saudi society and sensitivity toward Saudi regional and Arab concerns.

[1] For a discussion of partnership as a viable model for future relations between the United States and the Arab countries, see Nakhleh, *Arab-American Relations in the Persian Gulf*, pp. 68-82.

(2) Continued relative domestic political stability in Saudi Arabia, allowing sufficient time for gradual political reform and for Saudi society to absorb its hundreds of new college graduates and to adjust to the new ideas they will bring home from abroad.

(3) Development of a process of institutionalization of national policy so that agreements would cease to be the personal project of any one strong individual in government.

(4) Regional peace and the free flow of international trade.

(5) Open communication between the two countries on a regular basis regarding the changing elements of national interest as perceived by either state; each country must remain aware of the actual process of decision making within the other society.

The United States and Saudi Arabia have expressed active interest in and support of these five prerequisites. In terms of future relations, consideration should perhaps be given to the following areas:

(1) Saudi Arabia and the United States possess the power and influence to initiate a process of peace throughout the region by which both countries, as well as other countries in the region, would reap mutual benefits. Since the interests of the two countries are supplementary and not contradictory, Saudi Arabia and the United States possess the necessary qualifications for a lasting relationship. To bring this partnership to fruition, both countries must be willing to display open-mindedness, courage and creativity.

(2) It is clearly in the best interests of both countries to expend every effort to bring about a peaceful resolution of the outstanding regional conflicts. Among these conflicts, the Palestine question and the Dhufari rebellion stand out. Concerning Palestine, efforts should be directed toward the establishment of a Palestinian state in a part of Palestine. Supported by Saudi Arabia and the United States, such a Palestinian state could be a stabilizing factor in regional politics. No real stability can be expected in the region unless the Palestine conflict is resolved. Concerning the Dhufari rebellion, the United States and Saudi Arabia should propose a conference on the question of Dhufar involving Saudi Arabia, the Sultanate of Oman, the Popular Front for the Liberation of Oman and the People's Democratic Republic of Southern Yemen. The autonomy of Dhufar should be a priority topic on the agenda of the proposed conference, and the conference should convene under the auspices of the United Nations.

In addition to these options which are already in the implementation stage, American policy makers should, on a priority basis, require feasibility studies in the following areas:

(1) The long-term impact of the arms race in the Persian Gulf.

(2) The long-term relationship between American interests and the changing political nature of gulf societies.

(3) The durability of the present regimes and the impact of the new middle class on the American posture in the region.

(4) The usefulness of such bilateral agreements as the one on the naval facility in Bahrain.

(5) The long-term predictability of the political behavior of the present regional leadership, particularly in Saudi Arabia and Iran.

(6) The nature of long-term gulf security in the light of the developing relations between Iraq, Iran, and Saudi Arabia.

(7) The possibility of establishing friendly relations with Iraq.

(8) The long-term United States role in a peaceful solution of the Palestine conflict.

The United States has important and complex interests in the Middle East. American relations with Saudi Arabia, if based on far-sightedness, courage, and thorough knowledge of the region and its problems, can contribute significantly toward promoting these interests. Cold-war policy assumptions, which have been the basis of American strategic planning for the last twenty-five years, are no longer adequate. If the United States hopes to maintain an authoritative world position in the last two decades of this century, then American policy makers must have the wisdom and courage to make hard decisions in the 1970s.

Cover and book design: Pat Taylor